DRESSING DOLLS

Other Books by the Author
THE ART of MAKING CLOTH TOYS
THE ART of PUPPETS and MARIONETTES
TOYS: A STEP-BY-STEP GUIDE to CREATIVE TOYMAKING

DRESSING DOLLS

Clothing Patterns for
Rag, Baby, Toddler,
Older Action and
Fashion Dolls, and
Many, Many Others

Charlene Davis Roth

Photography: James A. Davis

Crown Publishers, Inc., New York

This book is dedicated to
William and Sally Roth
and Seymour Linker

Inquiries should be addressed to Crown Publishers, Inc., One Park Avenue,
New York, N.Y. 10016
Printed in the United States of America
Published simultaneously in Canada by
General Publishing Company Limited

Designed by Laurie Zuckerman

Library of Congress Cataloging in Publication Data

Roth, Charlene Davis, 1945-
 Dressing dolls.

  Includes index.
  1. Doll clothes.   I.   Title.
TT175.7.R67   745.59'22   76-801
 ISBN 0-517-52393-0
 ISBN 0-517-52394-9 pbk.

Contents

Introduction

Dolls are wonderful toys. They come alive in the hands of a child, invested with spirit and imagination. For a younger child, a doll is a friend and companion. To an older child dolls can help explore a world of adventure and romance. In all cases, dolls need clothing. A change of outfit gives it a whole new personality. Clothing is not only decorative: it can be a teaching device. Children can learn the fundamentals of dressing and undressing, how to open and close buttons and snaps, and so on.

Using the fundamentals outlined in the first two chapters you can make clothes for an infinite number of dolls: rag dolls, walking dolls, any kind of doll. You can make replicas of current fashions, antique doll clothing, or unique creations of your own. Or you can use the specific patterns given in this book for outfits ranging from everyday attire to gowns for a princess and costumes for a ballerina. Doll dressing is a pleasant and relaxing pastime. In a very short time you will develop the skills to assemble the tiny costumes, and to design your own creations.

Making, Altering, and Interpreting Patterns (1)

The patterns for doll clothing in this book are full size, and were designed for specific dolls that can be found in most stores. At the beginning of each chapter I have listed the name of the doll and the exact measurements for it. If you are using that particular doll, the patterns in that chapter need no alterations or adjustments. If, however, your doll has different measurements, the patterns must be altered. It is a very simple matter to do this.

First, measure your own doll and check the measurements against the ones listed. Mark down the measurements that vary. To alter the pattern, copy it from the book freehand, or using carbon paper. One at a time, erase the pattern lines that don't match your doll's measurements. Then redraw them, keeping the same shapes, but adjusting the lengths.

If, for example, your doll's leg is 2 inches longer than the one given in the book, erase the base of the pattern leg and add 2 inches to the sides of the leg, then redraw the base. Use the same procedure to make a pattern smaller, or narrower, or larger.

However, your doll's measurement may vary so completely from the one in the book that the pattern given is of no use to you. Or you may want to design your own pattern, using the outfits in the book as a reference point. Patternmaking is a craft in itself, and, like puzzle making, it involves drawing a number of shapes which will fit neatly together. At first glance it may seem a difficult task to tackle, but it is really a very simple procedure. The same basic shapes are repeated over and over. It is simply a matter of carefully measuring each shape and reproducing the measurements on paper. In any case, whether you use the patterns in the book and make only minor alterations, or you design your own patterns, the following information should be studied before you begin to make the doll outfits presented in this book.

Patternmaking Tools

The most important patternmaking tools are a *ruler* and *tape measure*. The tape is used to measure the doll, and the ruler to draw the lines of the pattern. You will also find it a good investment to buy a *curve template* to aid in drawing armholes and other curved edges. Besides the ruler, tape measure, and template, you will need a *pencil* with an *eraser, paper* (such as newsprint), and *scissors*. You will also need *tracing paper* to transcribe and alter patterns.

1-1 Tools necessary for patternmaking

Measuring

Measurement is the key to patternmaking. If you measure correctly and transcribe the measurements accurately to your drawing, the pattern pieces will fit together and the finished garment will fit the doll. For each kind of garment (shirt, dress, pants, shoes), specific parts of the doll's body must be measured and coordinated. For example: to make a pattern for a simple blouse (without set-in sleeves) it is necessary to design two pattern pieces, a front and a back. Using a tape measure you measure and write down:
   The length of the arm from shoulder to the wrist.
   The circumference of the arm at its widest point.
   The width of the shoulder where the arm joins to the neck.
   The circumferences of the neck and chest at their broadest points.
   The length from the shoulder to the center of the abdomen.

Other measurements necessary to make different articles of clothing include the length and circumference of the leg, circumference of the hip, size of the foot, circumference of the head, and so on. Also keep in mind the following considerations. An extra 1/4 inch must be added to each edge where there will be a seam. Also add approximately 1/2 inch to measurements such as the chest and circumference of the arm to ensure a roomy fit. Edges that are to be hemmed, like the base of a blouse or the ends of sleeves, require an additional 1/2 inch of fabric.

Drawing a Pattern

After you measure the doll, you have to translate the measurements into a drawing. It is a very simple procedure. Look at Figure 1-2, showing a blouse pattern, front and back. Dots and arrows indicate where each measurement was used.
   Sleeve length was determined by measuring the length of the doll's arm and adding 1/2 inch for a hem. I put dots (A) and (B) on the paper and connected them with a ruler.

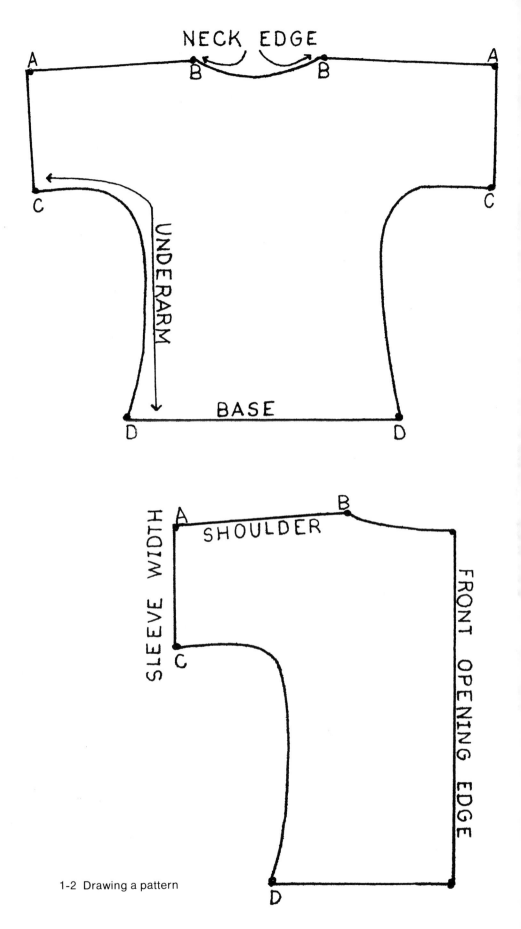

NECK EDGE

UNDERARM

BASE

SLEEVE WIDTH

SHOULDER

FRONT OPENING EDGE

1-2 Drawing a pattern

3

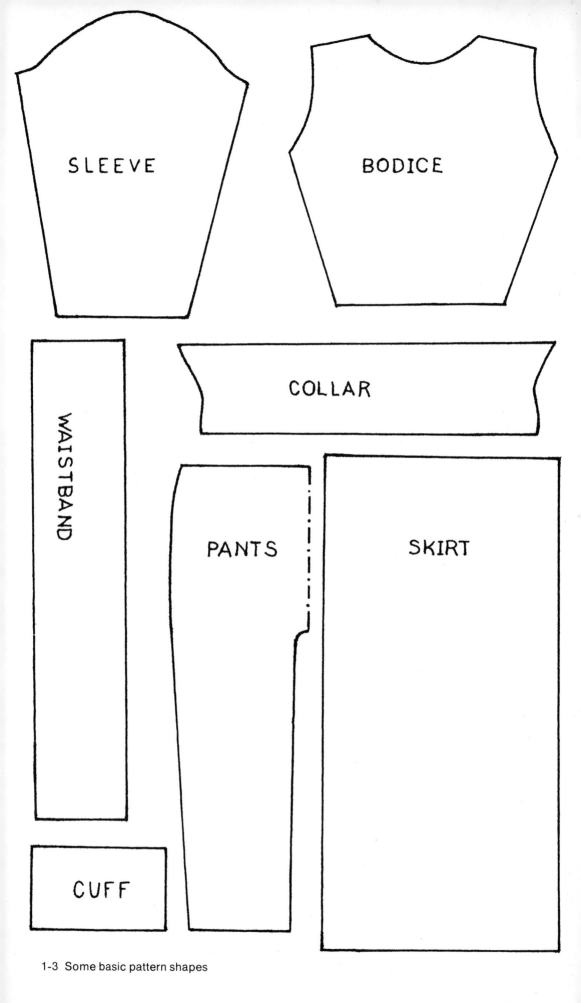

1-3 Some basic pattern shapes

Sleeve width was determined by dividing the circumference of the arm in half and adding 1/2 inch for roominess and 1/4 inch for each seam. I put dots (C) on the paper and connected them with (A).

Base width was determined by dividing the circumference of the hips in half and adding 1/2 inch for roominess and 1/4 inch for each seam. I put dots (D) on the paper and connected the base line. Then, with a curved edge, I drew in the underarm line and the neck edge.

Although the blouse pattern is simple, the principle for complex patterns is the same. Collars, set-in sleeves, waistbands, and other more intricate clothing pieces are only variations of basic shapes, and the procedures are the same. Figure 1-3 illustrates some of these basic pattern pieces. Keep in mind that two edges to be joined must be of equal length, even if one is curved and the other straight: the armhole edge and the curve of the sleeve should be equal in length; the straight edge of the collar and the neckline of a blouse should be of equal length whatever the shape of the collar.

Pattern Markings

A number of signs and symbols are marked on the patterns. They are guides to help you assemble the clothes. The markings must be transferred from the patterns to the fabric before stitching, a procedure explained in chapter 2.

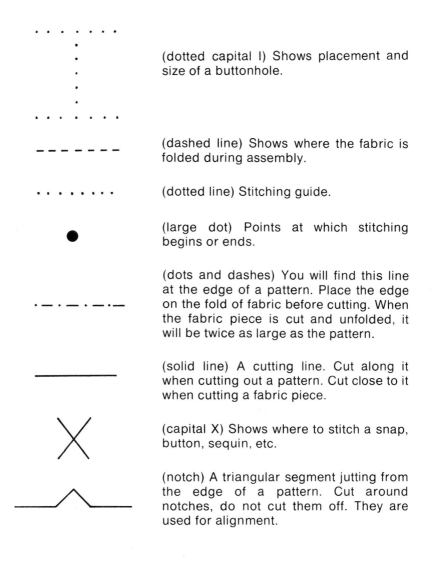

(dotted capital I) Shows placement and size of a buttonhole.

(dashed line) Shows where the fabric is folded during assembly.

(dotted line) Stitching guide.

(large dot) Points at which stitching begins or ends.

(dots and dashes) You will find this line at the edge of a pattern. Place the edge on the fold of fabric before cutting. When the fabric piece is cut and unfolded, it will be twice as large as the pattern.

(solid line) A cutting line. Cut along it when cutting out a pattern. Cut close to it when cutting a fabric piece.

(capital X) Shows where to stitch a snap, button, sequin, etc.

(notch) A triangular segment jutting from the edge of a pattern. Cut around notches, do not cut them off. They are used for alignment.

② Techniques, Tools, and Fabrics

All the outfits presented in the following chapters are assembled by following the same procedures. First the patterns are copied from the book and altered if necessary (chapter 1). Then the fabrics are cut and marked. The cut pieces are sewn together. Next the surface of the garment is finished (buttons, closures, trims, etc.). Before I explain the assembly procedures in detail, a discussion of fabrics is in order.

Fabrics. In the book I have suggested loose guidelines for the types of fabrics and color patterns you can use for each outfit. But other fabrics and designs may be equally suitable, and the final choice is left to you. However, if I specify knit fabrics, do not substitute a fabric that does not stretch (certain patterns require stretch to obtain an accurate fit). Also, when I call for a *yard* of fabric, I mean the piece must be 36 inches long and *at least* 36 inches wide.

Doll clothes are subjected to a great deal of wear and tear. Fabrics which pull apart easily or fray extensively will not withstand a child's play. Use quality fabrics: I am not saying you have to use heavyweight fabrics; many seemingly delicate fabrics are quite sturdy. Check labels to be sure the materials are colorfast and washable.

Another thing to keep in mind when choosing fabrics is that dolls are generally small. Therefore choose small prints and patterns that won't overwhelm a small doll (though large loud prints or plaids may be suitable for a baby's rag doll, where color is more important than the illusion of reality).

The yardage necessary for making doll clothing is small. You can use leftover scraps of fabric from large-size shirts or other sewing projects. And you can always salvage usable fabrics from outgrown or out-of-style clothing. Even the smallest scrap of fabric can be useful for a doll garment. Another source of fabrics is the remnant counter. Often 1/4 or 1/8 yard of fabric offered at reduced price will make a nice ensemble for a doll.

A list of fabrics and their properties is found below.

Cotton: This natural fabric comes in a variety of weights, textures, and colors. The surface may be glossy, smooth, rough, or napped. It is useful for everything from pinafores and undergarments to gowns, slacks, and coats. It may be colorfast and washable.

Fake Fur or Pile: These man-made fabrics are characterized by their nap. The naps vary in length and are attached to a knitted backing. They make nice snowsuits, imitation fur coats, and the like. They can be obtained in a variety of colors or patterns that imitate animal furs.

Felt: This is a pressed rather than a knitted or woven fabric. Because it is pressed, it will not fray and the edges need not be finished. This property makes it useful for hats, shoes, appliqués, vests, and other articles with unfinished edges. Buy a good quality of felt as the cheaper stuff tends to pull apart too easily to be of value for doll clothing.

Knits: Knits are constructed from interlocking loops as opposed to weaving. They are stretchy and flexible, making them a good choice for doll clothing. They also come in a wide range of colors, prints, and textures.

Lace and Net: Lace and net fabrics are held together by a series of knots. Plain patterns, like fishnets, make excellent underskirts, while the beautiful lace fabrics are ideal for fancy pinafores and gowns.

Silk, Satin, Taffeta: I have grouped these fabrics together because of their lustrous surfaces and pliable qualities. They are useful for making fancy evening wear or delicate lingerie.

Velvet and Velveteen: Both these fabrics have short, silky naps. Velvet is usually made from silk, velveteen from cotton. They are plushy and luxurious, yet sturdy. They work well for a variety of dressy garments ranging from jackets to pants suits to gowns.

ASSEMBLY TECHNIQUES

Tracing. To trace the patterns directly from the book you will need a *pencil* and *tracing paper.* Place the tracing paper over the pattern and copy it. Be sure to trace all the pattern markings (dots, dashes, solid lines, Xs, etc.). Also transfer to the paper the name of the piece (Bodice Front, Shoe Upper, etc.) and the number of pieces to be cut (Cut Two, Cut One, etc.). Alter the patterns if necessary.

Ironing and Pinning. You will need an *iron, ironing board, straight pins, pin holder.* Always press the fabrics before you pin on the patterns. Unpressed fabrics do not cut accurately. One wrinkle can change the fit of a piece. After ironing, pin the patterns to the fabric. If the pattern shows a line of alternating dots and dashes, fold the fabric and pin this line along the fold. Remember to pin patterns to napped fabrics so the nap will run in the same direction on all garment pieces. Fabrics with one-way designs also require special placement of pattern pieces.

Cutting. You will need *scissors.* Seven-inch dressmaker's scissors can be used for most of the cutting, but I prefer 5-inch scissors for greater cutting accuracy, especially on small pieces. Occasionally you will be instructed to cut a rectangle of fabric for which there is not a pattern in the book. Simply use the measurements given, draw the rectangle on a sheet of paper and cut it for a pattern, then pin it to the fabric and cut. Don't remove the patterns after you cut the fabric until you have transferred the markings, the next procedural step.

Transferring Markings. To transfer the markings to the fabric you will need *dressmaker's tracing paper* (you can buy it at any notions counter or fabric store). A *tracing wheel* is also helpful, or a blunt instrument, like a knitting needle or pencil that's not sharp enough to pierce the paper or pattern.

Pattern markings (discussed in chapter 1) must be transferred from the patterns to the fabric. If you are transferring markings to a light color fabric, use dark tracing paper. If the fabric is dark, use a light color of paper. Refer to Figure 2-1. Sandwich a sheet of tracing paper between the fabric and the pattern. The colored side of the tracing paper should be against the fabric. Pin the pattern, tracing

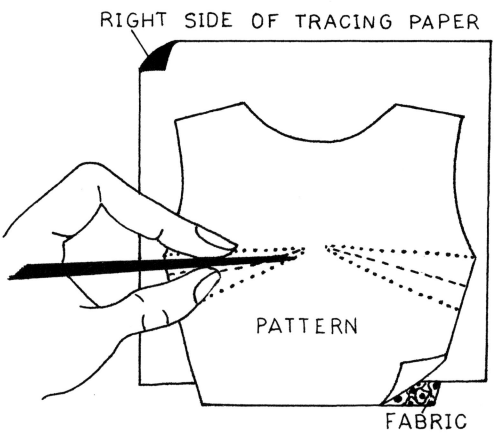

RIGHT SIDE OF TRACING PAPER

PATTERN

FABRIC

2-1 Transferring markings from a pattern to the fabric

paper, and fabric together. Trace over the markings on the pattern with a tracing wheel or blunt marking instrument. Use just enough pressure to get a recognizable mark on the fabric. When tracing is finished, remove the pins and pattern and check to be sure all the markings were transferred accurately.

Sewing. When you sew you join two or more edges of fabric with a length of thread. You can sew by hand or machine. Sewing by machine is faster. Any sewing machine that sews a tight, straight stitch will do to make the doll clothes in this book. A machine that also stitches zigzag is helpful for finishing seams and decorating the garments, but not essential. Check your machine manual for proper settings for the different fabrics you will be using. A ball-point machine needle helps to sew slippery knits and treated fabrics.

One quarter inch of fabric is allowed for the *seams* of the garments in this book. Most sewing machines have a measuring guide on the throat plate that helps to determine seam width. *Half an inch* of fabric is allotted on edges to be *hemmed* (except when narrower hems are specified, then use 1/4 inch of fabric). Most hems on small articles of clothing should be stitched by hand. Unless it is specifically stated in the assembly instructions, a garment is always stitched with *right* sides of the fabric together.

When choosing thread, try to match it to the color of the fabric you are sewing. I prefer polyester sewing thread for machine and hand sewing because it is strong and flexible. Clear nylon thread is also

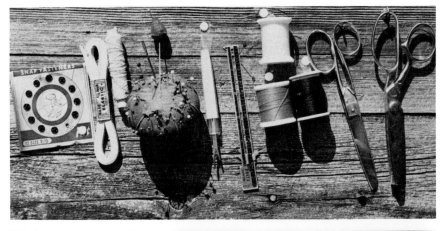
2-2 Sewing equipment

2-3 Trims

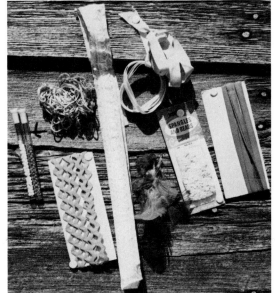

useful, especially for surface sewing such as attaching closures and trims. It blends with different colors and is strong. But nylon thread is sometimes difficult to handle, so run a length of it against a piece of wax before threading a needle.

Because doll clothing usually receives rough handling, it is important to finish a seam properly. After stitching a seam, press it open. Use a zigzag stitch and stitch along each of the raw edges of the seam. Or pink the raw edges with pinking shears. Press the stitched clothing before proceeding.

Finishing. Snap closures, buttons, or ties are often attached to a garment to hold it on the doll. These closures can be interchanged. If your child is young and likely to bite off a button and swallow it, use ribbon ties. For children who are too young to tie a bow, but old enough to change doll clothing, substitute a strap that snaps or buttons to the fabrics. All closures are subject to stress: stitch them *securely* to the fabric.

Trims offer a seamstress the chance to show creativity. They are found in a limitless variety and can be used in infinite ways. The addition of trim can make a doll outfit unique. Here is a list with a few ideas for the application.

Appliqués: Embroidered patches of felt or other fabric appliqués can be sewn to the surface of a garment and used to decorate jackets, pockets, pant legs, or the bodice of dresses.

Beads: They come in many colors and sizes, either plain or variegated. Stitch them singly to the fabric surface or in patterns. Use nylon thread.

Bias Tape: Contrasting colors of bias tape can be used to bind edges for a decorative finish.

Braid: Narrow braid comes in many woven patterns and colors, including metallic gold and silver. It works well as an outline for the front of a blouse or jacket, or as a finish for the base of a skirt, trouser legs, sleeves, or neck edge.

Buttons: Buttons can be used for decoration as well as for closure. Stitch them to cuffs, shoulders, or down the front of a dress.

Embroidery: Colorful embroidered designs make a very pretty addition to the surface of doll clothing.

Feathers: Small colorful feathers can be used to spruce up a cap or bonnet. Stitch them securely to the fabric.

Fringe: Fringe can be stitched to the base of skirts, jackets, and vests, along the underarm seam or across the front of a blouse or jacket. It is colorful and mobile, adding an interesting touch.

Lace and Ruffles: Lace comes in a wide variety of designs, colors, and widths. I usually use a 1/4-inch-wide gathered lace edging to trim doll clothes. It adds a delicate touch to baby doll clothing and makes fashion doll outfits stylish.

Ribbon: Ribbon can be used for ties, waistbands, and decorative bows. Choose a width to suit the size of the garment. Both satin and grosgrain ribbon come in many pretty colors.

Rhinestones: These sparkling little stones make a gown truly eye-catching. You can stitch them one at a time or in patterns. A rhinestone setter makes the work go much faster.

Rickrack: This zigzag-shaped woven fabric trim can be hand or machine stitched to the surface of a garment. It comes in several colors and widths.

Sequins: These colorful shiny little metallic circles can be stitched to the fabric by hand in various patterns or designs.

Stitching: Topstitching, zigzag, or other fancy stitches can be used effectively for decoration. Choose a color of thread that contrasts or highlights the fabric. Stitch along the edges of hems or seams for interesting effects.

Yarn: Yarn can be used as an alternative to ribbon when making ties, waistbands, and bows.

Dressing the Baby Doll  3

The baby clothes in this chapter have been designed for a Madame Alexander doll named Sweet Tears. Here are her measurements: height, 11 inches; chest, 7 1/2 inches; hips, 9 1/2 inches; length of arm, 4 inches; length of inner leg, 3 1/2 inches; circumference of head, 10 inches. Carefully measure your own doll and compare those measurements with those given above. If the measurements vary, alter the patterns to fit following the instructions given in chapter 1.

DIAPER, T-SHIRT

For a diaper and T-shirt a white cotton knit with or without ribs is your best choice of fabric. You don't have to buy the fabric: use a clean old T-shirt from the rag pile.

MATERIALS

1/3 yard of white cotton knit fabric for the T-shirt
   and diaper.
One size 00 snap closure for the T-shirt.
Two 1-inch safety pins or two size 00 snap closures
   to fasten the diaper.
White thread.

3-1 Diaper and T-shirt

Diaper. Press the fabric and cut a rectangle measuring 8 1/2 x 10 inches. By hand or machine, narrowly hem each of the four raw edges of the rectangle. Press the hemmed fabric and then fold the diaper as you would for a baby. Pin it around the doll, or substitute snap closures stitched to the fabric if the child you are making the outfit for is too young to open and close a safety pin.

T-shirt. Using the pattern in Figure 3-2 as a guide, cut two pieces of white fabric for the front and back of the T-shirt. Transfer the X marked at the neck to the *wrong* side of *one* piece and to the *right* side of the remaining piece.

Align the two pieces then stitch the shoulder seams and the under-arm seams (Figure 3-3). Narrowly hem the neck edge, the ends of the sleeves, and the base of the garment. Stitch half of the snap closure to each point marked X. *

---

*Another traditional baby garment is the bib. Refer to chapter 4 and make a bib, using the pattern and instructions for making the apron which decorates the gingham dress.

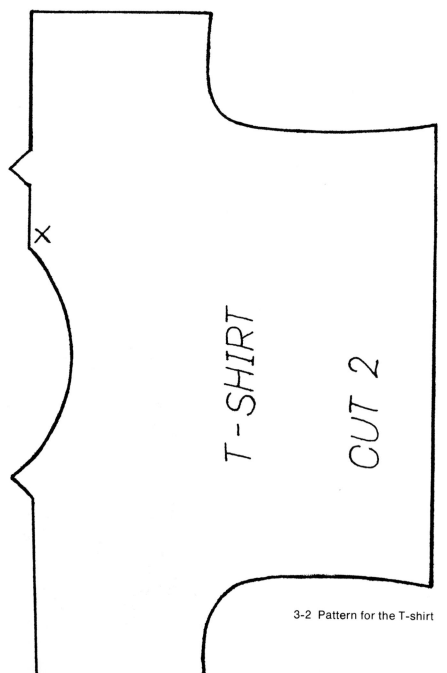

3-2 Pattern for the T-shirt

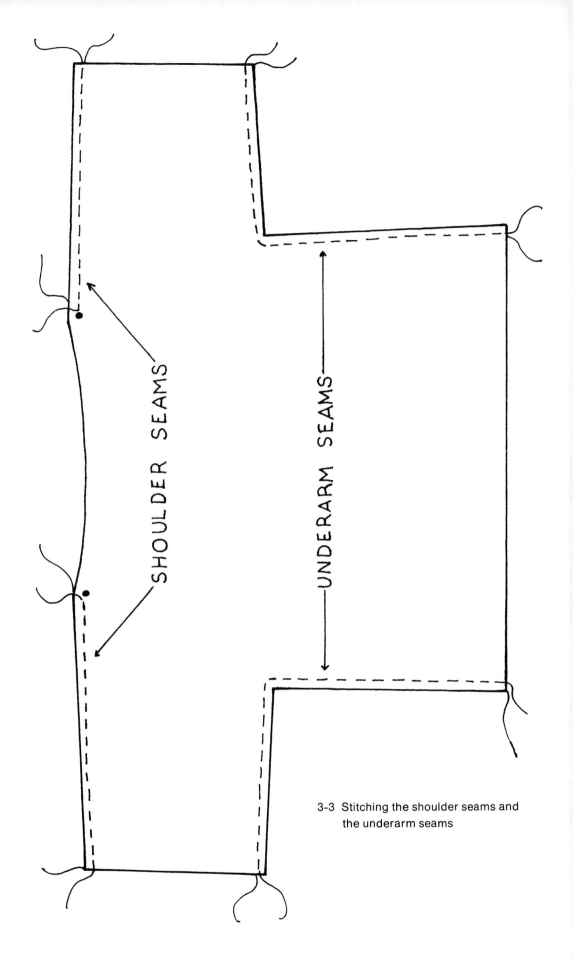

SHOULDER SEAMS

UNDERARM SEAMS

3-3 Stitching the shoulder seams and
the underarm seams

FOOTED PAJAMAS

These two-piece sleepers are easy to slip on and off. The bottoms have an elasticized waist, and the top ties simply at the throat with two lengths of ribbon.

MATERIALS

1/3 yard of printed cotton flannel for the pajama
  tops, bottoms, and feet.
An 8-inch length of 1/4-inch-wide elastic.
Two lengths of 1/4-inch-wide satin ribbon, each
  measuring 6 1/2 inches.
Thread to match the fabric.

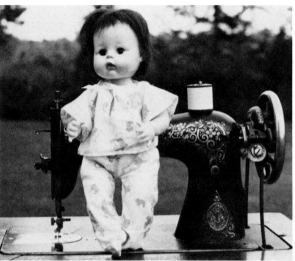

3-4 Baby Doll Pajamas

Figure 3-5 a + b shows the patterns for the footed pajamas. Cut two tops, two bottoms, and four foot pieces. Transfer the X to the wrong side of *one* top piece. Transfer all other markings to the wrong side of the fabric.

Begin the pajama bottoms by attaching a foot to each leg. Refer to Figure 3-6, which illustrates this procedure. With right sides of the fabric together, align the *notched* edge of the foot and leg. Stitch the edges together. Repeat, stitching a foot to each leg. Press the assembled pieces flat.

Align the two bottom pieces and stitch one side seam together from the waist to the toe. Press the piece open and flat. Turn, press and stitch to the inside 1/4 inch of fabric along the waist edge. Turn an additional 1/2 inch of fabric to the inside and stitch close to both edges of this folded piece to create a casing for elastic (Figure 3-7). Thread the 8-inch length of elastic through the casing, stitching it securely to both ends of the casing.

Stitch the second side seam from the waist to the toe. Stitch the crotch seam, stitching the sides of the feet closed as you proceed. Turn the bottoms right side out and press.

Next take the top piece marked with an X on the wrong side of the fabric and cut a slit from the neck edge to the X. This slit is large enough to allow the doll's head to pass through.

With right sides together, align the front and back pieces. Stitch the shoulder seams and the underarm seams (Figure 3-3). Narrowly hem the neck edge, the edges of the slit, the ends of the sleeves, and the base of the top. Press and turn right side out.

Stitch a 6 1/2-inch length of ribbon to the inside upper edge of each side of the slit. Put the top on the doll and tie the ribbon in a bow to hold the neck opening closed.

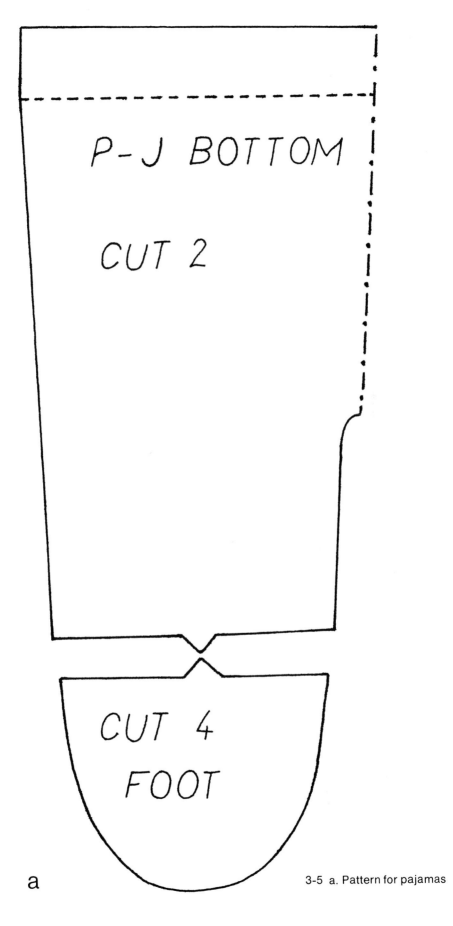

P-J BOTTOM

CUT 2

CUT 4

FOOT

a

3-5 a. Pattern for pajamas

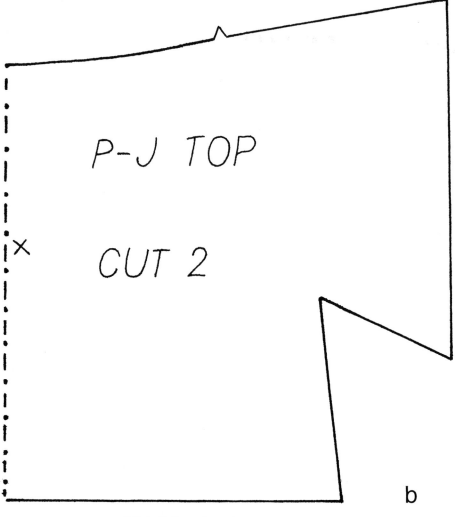

P-J TOP

CUT 2

×

b

3-5 b. Pattern for pajamas

3-6 Attaching a foot to the leg of the pajama bottom

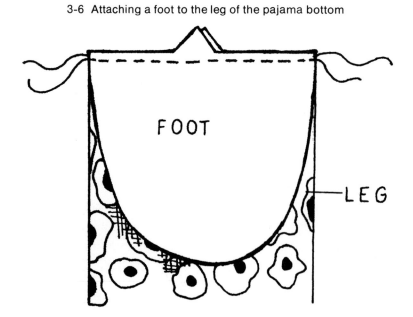

FOOT

LEG

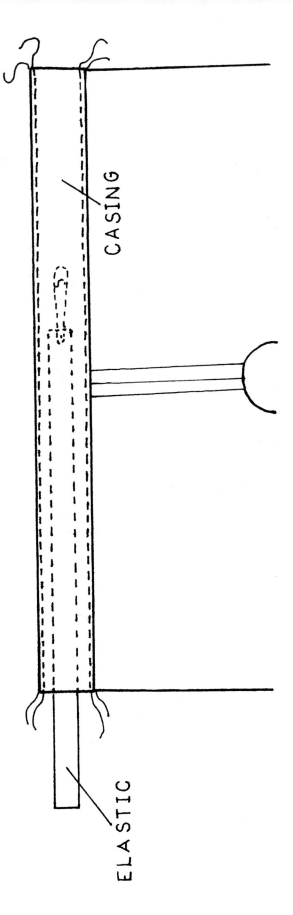

3-7 Creating a casing for elastic

HOODED BATH TOWEL, RECEIVING BLANKET

Every child enjoys taking a washable doll into the tub, especially when the doll has its own towel and a nice blanket with which to wrap it when dry. These two garments are easy to cut and sew, yet will receive as much play as more complicated pieces.

MATERIALS

1/3 yard of terry cloth fabric for the towel, hood,
   and a washcloth.
2/3 yard of cotton flannel for the receiving blanket.
Thread to match the fabrics.

3-8 Towel and Receiving Blanket

Hooded Towel. To begin the hooded towel, cut a rectangle of terry cloth measuring 12 x 14 inches. Using the hood pattern in Figure 3-9 for a guide, cut one hood from terry cloth. If you want to make a washcloth, cut a 5-inch square from the same fabric.

With right sides of the fabric together, align and stitch the notched edges of the hood to the towel (Figure 3-10). Turn the hood right side out and hem the unstitched edge. Also hem the remaining raw edges of the towel. Press and the towel is completed.

To make the washcloth simply hem the four unfinished edges and press.

Receiving Blanket. For the blanket, cut a rectangle of fabric measuring 24 x 36 inches. To finish it, either hem by hand or overedge stitch by machine each of the four raw edges. For a fancier finish, the edges may be bound with grosgrain ribbon or bias tape (instructions and a diagram for this procedure are detailed in Figure 4-7).

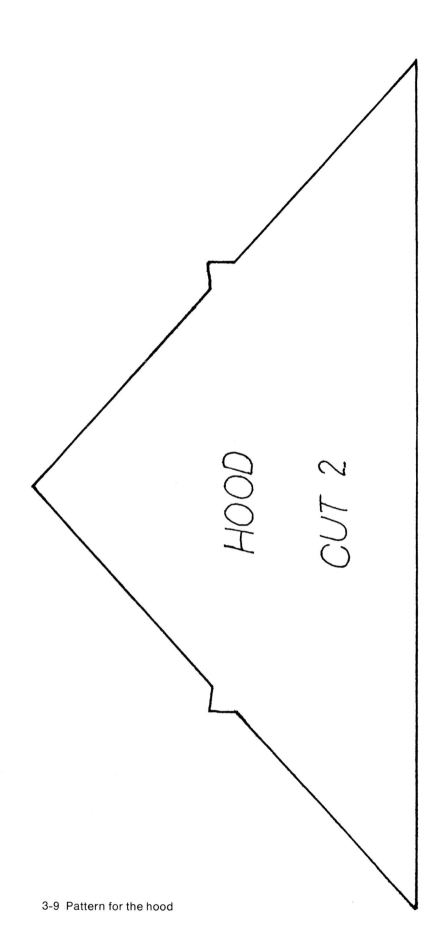

3-9 Pattern for the hood

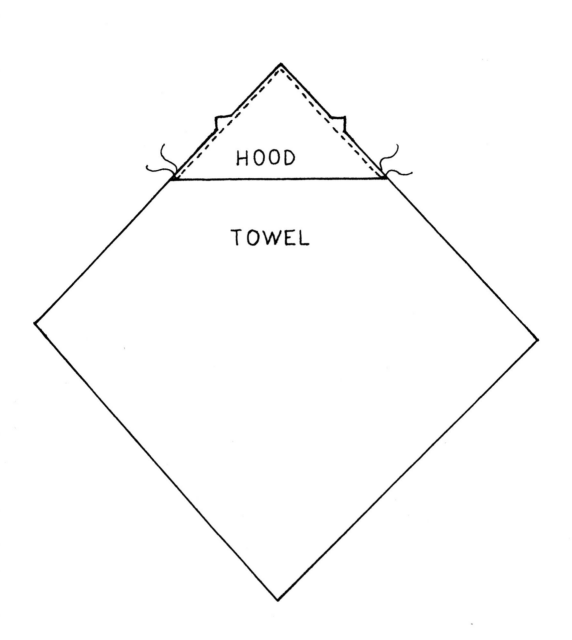

3-10 Stitching the hood to the towel

SWEATER, BONNET, BOOTIES

These three cozy articles of clothing must be cut from a stretchable sweater-knit fabric to obtain an accurate fit. You can buy the material at a fabric store or cut the pieces from a sweater no longer in use.

MATERIALS

1/3 yard of stretchable knit fabric for the sweater,
  bonnet, and booties.
A 15-inch length of 1/2-inch-wide gathered lace
  edging for the bonnet.
A 20-inch length of 1/4-inch-wide satin ribbon for
  bonnet ties.
A 20-inch length of rug yarn for bootie ties.
Two buttons with 1/4-inch diameters.
Thread to match the fabric.

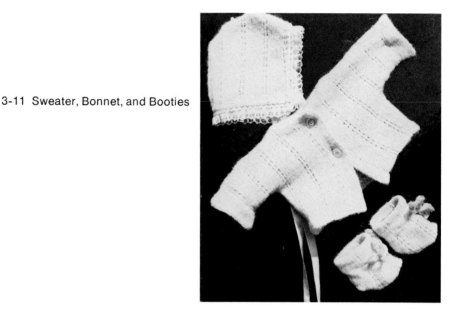

3-11 Sweater, Bonnet, and Booties

Use the patterns for the sweater front, back, bonnet, and booties (Figure 3-12 a and b). Be sure to place marked edges on the fold before cutting. Cut two bonnet pieces, two booties, two sweater fronts, and one sweater back. Transfer markings to the *wrong* side of the fabric except for the slashes on the booties and the buttonhole markings which are to be transferred to the *right* side of the fabric.

Sweater. With right sides together, align one sweater front piece with the back piece and stitch the shoulder seam from the end of the sleeve to the neck edge. Stitch the underarm seam of these same two pieces (Figure 3-3). Stitch the second sweater front piece to the back. Hem the neck edge, the front opening edges, the ends of the sleeves, and the base of the sweater.

By hand or machine make buttonholes at the two points marked on the right sweater front. Stitch a tiny button to each of the points marked on the left sweater front. Press the finished sweater (place a damp cloth between the fabric and the iron when pressing sweater knit fabrics).

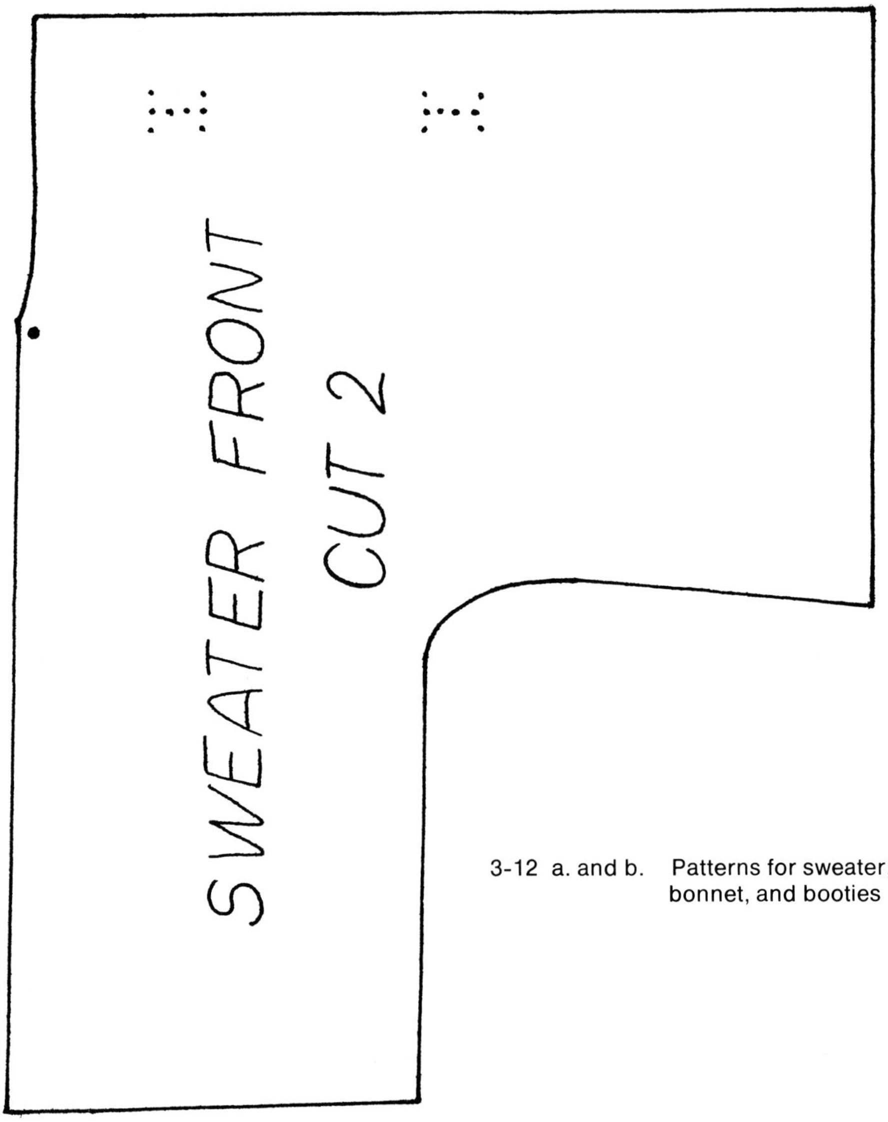

SWEATER FRONT
CUT 2

3-12 a. and b.   Patterns for sweater,
bonnet, and booties

a

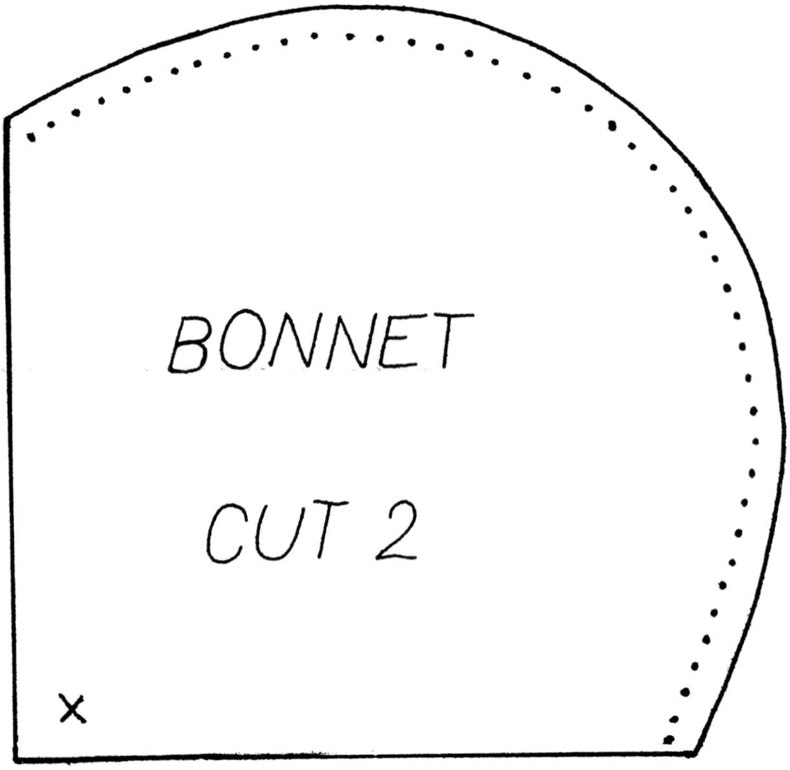

BONNET

CUT 2

X

SWEATER BACK
CUT 1

b

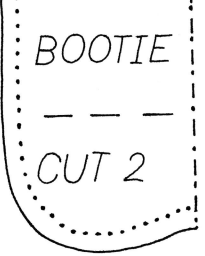

BOOTIE

CUT 2

Bonnet. Stitch the two bonnet pieces together, placing the line of stitching over the dotted line marked on the fabric. Hem the remaining unfinished edge of the bonnet. Stitch the length of gathered lace close to the hemmed edge so the lace extends beyond the fabric and forms a narrow brim. To finish, stitch a 10-inch length of satin ribbon to each inside corner of the bonnet at the point marked with an X.

Booties. Each bootie is constructed from a single piece of fabric. Fold one piece of fabric with right sides together (Figure 3-13a) and stitch over the marked dotted stitching line. Hem the upper raw edge. Turn the bootie right side out and press. Thread a 10-inch length of rug yarn from the front, in and out and through the fabric at the slashes (Figure 3-13b). To prevent the yarn drawstring from unraveling, knot the ends. Tie a bow at the front of the bootie. Assemble the second bootie.

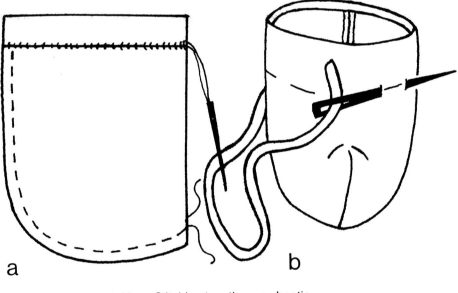

a   b

3-13 a. Stitching together one bootie
      b. Stitching yarn ties to the bootie

BIBBED OVERALLS, BLOUSE

Bibbed overalls are classic casual wear for babies. The ones shown are made of wool flannel, but cotton, denim, or any number of medium weight fabrics are suitable. The shirt is gingham-printed cotton.

MATERIALS

1/4 yard of cotton fabric for the blouse.
1/4 yard of fabric for the overalls.
Two size 00 snaps for the blouse.
Two buttons with 1/4-inch diameters for the
   overalls.
A 3-inch length of 1/4-inch-wide elastic for the
   overalls.
Thread to match the fabrics.

3-14 Bibbed Overalls and Blouse

The patterns for the blouse are shown in Figure 3-15a, b, and c. Cut one back and one front piece. Cut two strips of fabric 1 1/2 x 7 inches for the straps. Transfer markings for the buttonholes to the *right* side of the fabric. Transfer all other markings to the wrong side of the fabric.

Blouse. Begin by stitching one blouse front piece to the back piece at the shoulder seam (Figure 3-3). Stitch the underarm seam. Stitch the second blouse front to the back. Hem the ends of the sleeves, the front opening edges, and the base of the blouse.

Take one collar piece and press 1/4 inch of fabric along the straight edge to the inside (Figure 3-16a). Next align the two collar pieces (right sides together) and stitch the curved edge. Turn the piece right side out and press. Baste the right side of the unfolded straight edge of the collar to the wrong side of the blouse neck edge, then stitch where you have basted (Figure 3-16b). Press the seam toward the collar, then stitch the folded edge of the collar over the seam (Figure 3-16c).

Press the blouse. Stitch two snap closures to the front opening edges. Place one snap just below the collar and the second snap 2 inches below the first.

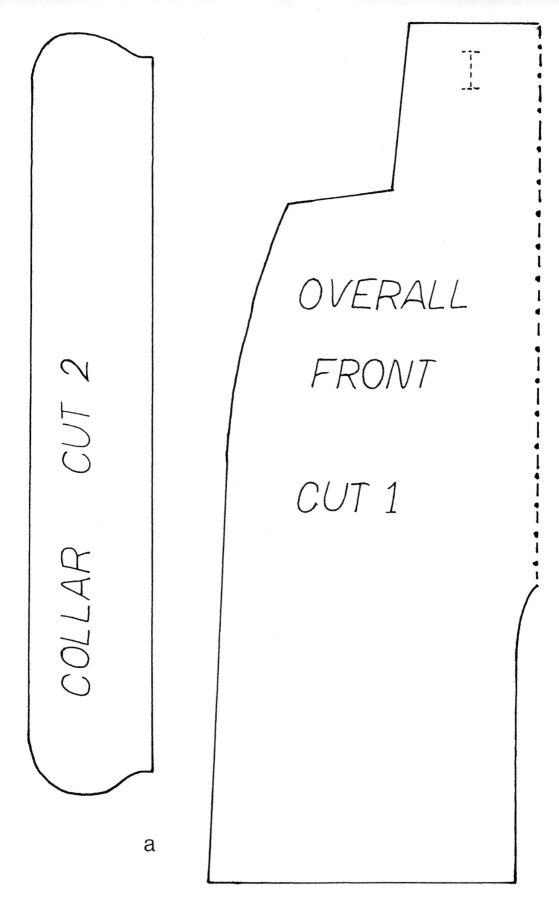

COLLAR CUT 2

OVERALL FRONT CUT 1

a

3-15 a, b, and c Patterns for bibbed overalls and blouse

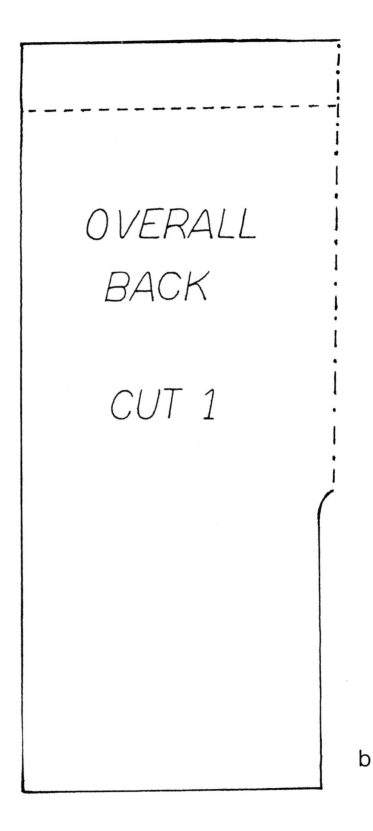

OVERALL

BACK

CUT 1

b

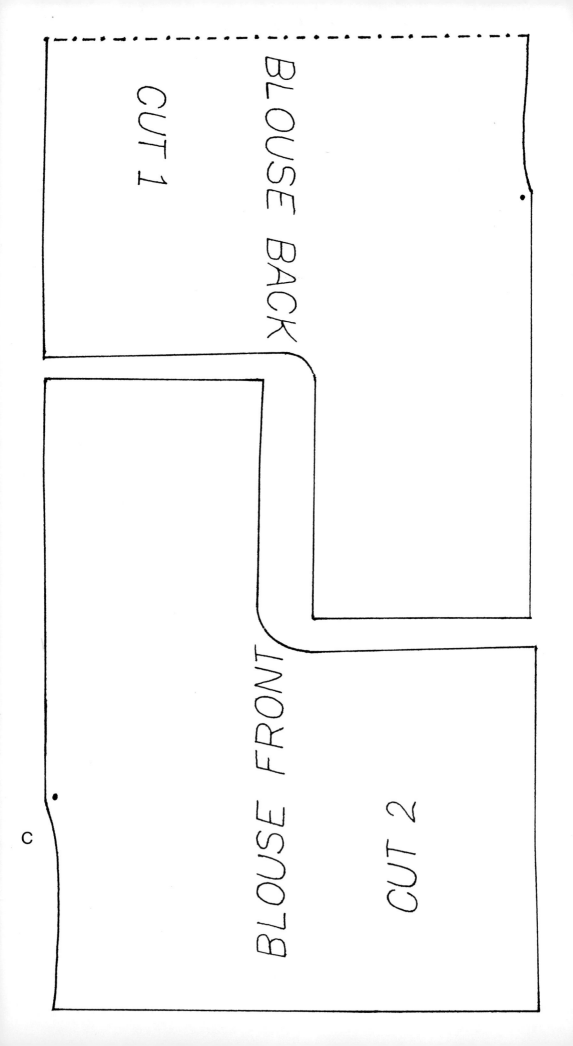

BLOUSE BACK

CUT 1

BLOUSE FRONT

CUT 2

c

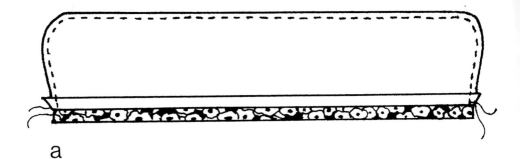

a

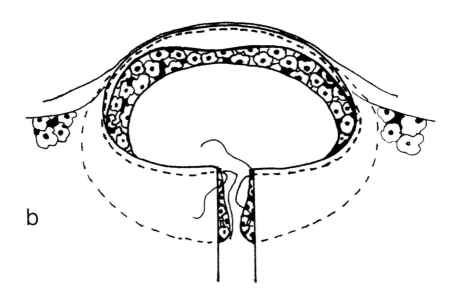

b

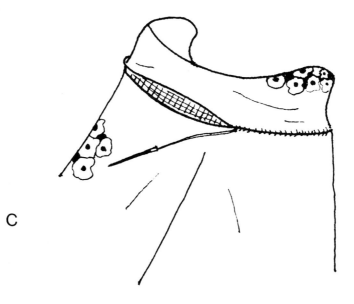

c

3-16 a. Stitching the curved edge of two collar pieces
together
b. Stitching one edge of the collar to the blouse
c. Stitching the folded edge of the collar over the
seam

Overalls. The overalls are gathered at the back waistband with elastic. To begin, turn to the inside and press 1/4 inch of fabric along the waist edge of the back overall. Stitch the edge in place. Turn an additional 1/2 inch of fabric to the inside, along the fold line marked on the fabric. Stitch close to both edges of this folded piece to form a casing for elastic (Figure 3-7). Thread the 3-inch length of 1/4-inch-wide elastic through the casing and stitch it securely to both ends of the casing.

Stitch the front of the overalls to the back at the side seams, stitching from the base of the legs to the waist. Stitch the crotch seam from the inside base of one leg around to the base of the second leg.

Hem the edges of the bib. This can be done by hand or by machine. If you want a nice decorative touch, use a contrasting color of thread and a zigzag stitch. Hem the base of the legs.

The straps are made from two strips of fabric. Take one strip then turn, press, and stitch to the inside 1/4 inch of fabric along each *long* edge. Fold the long way and press the strip in half, wrong sides together. Stitch close to both long edges of the folded piece. Hem the two short ends of the strip. Repeat and make the second strap. Stitch a strap to each side of the back waistband. Stitch a small button to the right side of the opposite ends of the straps.

To finish the overalls, by hand or machine make two buttonholes in the bib, placing each one at the points marked on the fabric. Press the garment, creasing each leg.

ROMPER SUIT, BONNET

The romper suit and bonnet are made from brightly printed cotton. This is a perfect outfit for a doll to wear when going to the beach, on a picnic, or to the zoo.

3-17 Romper Suit and Bonnet

MATERIALS

1/4 yard brightly printed cotton fabric for the
    romper suit and bonnet.
A 13-inch length of 1/4-inch-wide elastic for the
    suit.
An 8-inch length of 1/2-inch-wide gathered lace
    edging for the bonnet brim.
A 28-inch length of 1/4-inch-wide satin ribbon for
    ties.
Thread to match the fabrics.

Figure 3-18a and b shows the patterns for the bonnet and romper
suit. Cut one suit front piece, one back piece, and one facing piece.
Cut two side pieces and one strip for the bonnet. Transfer all markings to the wrong side of the fabrics.

Romper Suit. Begin the romper suit by turning to the inside 1/4
inch of the notched edge of the facing. Press and stitch this edge in
place. With right sides together, align the facing with the romper suit
bib. Stitch all but the hemmed edge of the facing to the suit. Turn the
facing to the inside and press. Topstitch 1/8 inch within the outer
edge of the bib.

To make the casing for the elastic waistband, turn 1/4 inch of the
back waist edge of the romper suit to the inside. Press and stitch in
place. Turn to the inside an additional 1/2 inch of fabric along this
edge. Stitch close to both edges of the folded piece to create a casing (Figure 3-7). Thread a 3-inch length of 1/4-inch-wide elastic
through this casing. Stitch the elastic to both ends of the casing.

Stitch the suit front to the back along the side seams. The legs of
the romper suit are elasticized. Follow the same procedure explained
above for the waistband and make a casing at the base of each leg.
Thread each casing with a 5-inch length of elastic. Stitch the ends of
the elastic to the ends of the casing. Stitch the crotch seam of the
suit.

Cut two 7-inch lengths of ribbon. Stitch one to each upper corner
of the bib facing. The ribbons are tied in a bow around the doll's neck
to hold the bib in place. Press the suit.

Bonnet. Begin by stitching the dart marked on the strip. Then,
baste one side of the strip to the notched edge of one bonnet piece
(Figure 3-19a). Stitch. Baste and stitch the second side of the strip to
the remaining bonnet piece.

Hem the raw edges of the bonnet. Stitch the gathered lace edging
to the front edge of the bonnet (Figure 3-19b). Hem the ends of the
lace. (If you don't have lace you can make a brim with a strip of fabric. Cut a piece of fabric 2 x 12 inches and fold the piece in half, right
sides together, so you have a long narrow piece. Stitch the raw edges
together. Turn the resulting tube right side out. Hem the raw ends.
Press. Run a basting stitch 1/8 inch within one long edge of the
piece. Gather the strip so it is 8 inches in length. Stitch over the
gathers to hold them in place. Stitch the gathered edge of the piece
to the front edge of the bonnet.)

Cut two 7-inch lengths of 1/4-inch-wide satin ribbon, and stitch a
length of ribbon to each inside front corner of the bonnet for ties.

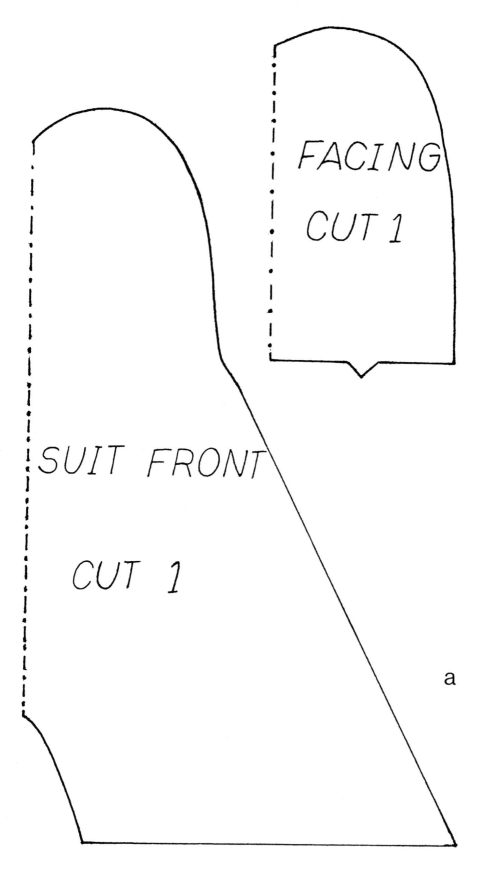

FACING

CUT 1

SUIT FRONT

CUT 1

a

3-18 a and b Patterns for romper suit and bonnet

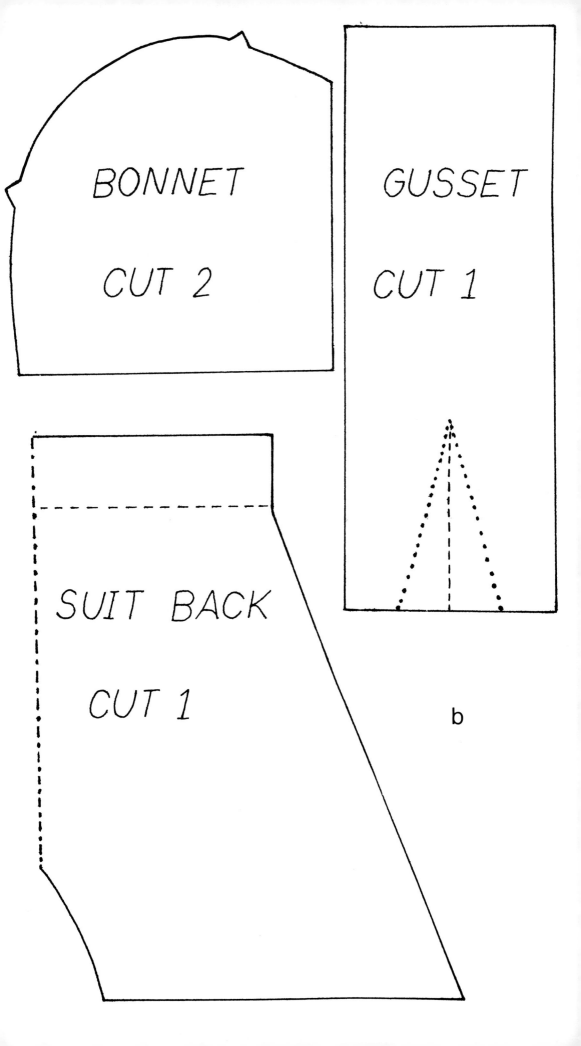

BONNET

CUT 2

GUSSET

CUT 1

SUIT BACK

CUT 1

b

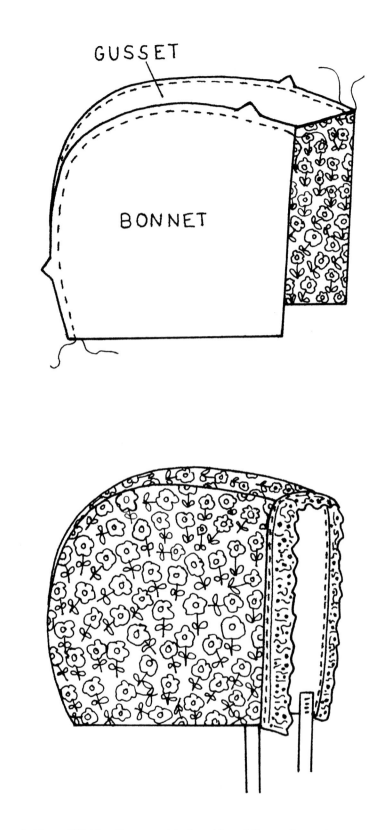

GUSSET

BONNET

a

b

3-19 a. Stitching the gusset to the sides of the sunbonnet
b. Attaching the lace brim and ribbon ties to the sunbonnet

SNOWSUIT

The snowsuit is cut from nappy fabric, such as pile or fake fur. Use one color for the main body and hood of the snowsuit and a contrasting color for the hood trim, mittens, and booties. Mittens, booties, and hood are attached, making the suit an all-in-one winter garment.

MATERIALS

1/3 yard of fur or pile fabric for the main body of the suit.
Scraps of contrasting color fabric for hood trim, mittens, and booties.
Four size 00 snaps to close the front.
A 16-inch length of 1/4-inch-wide satin ribbon for hood ties.
Thread to match the fabric.

3-20 Snowsuit

The patterns for the snowsuit can be found in Figure 3-21a and b. From pressed fabric cut two bodice front pieces, one bodice back, two pants pieces, and two hood pieces. From the contrasting color fabric cut four mitten pieces, four bootie pieces, and a strip measuring 2 x 10 1/2 inches for the hood trim. Transfer all markings to the wrong side of the fabric.

Refer to Figure 3-6, which shows how the foot is attached to the pajama bottoms. Following this same procedure, align the notched edge of a mitten piece with the notched edge of the base of one sleeve. Stitch the edges together. Stitch a mitten piece to each bodice sleeve and stitch a bootie piece to each leg. Press the pieces flat.

Now align the two hood pieces and stitch the pair together, placing the line of stitching over the dotted line marked on the fabric. Next take the strip for the hood trim, turn, press, and stitch 1/4 inch of fabric along one long edge to the inside. With right sides together, align the raw edge of the strip with the raw edge of the hood. Stitch the edges together. Press the seam toward the strip. Turn the hemmed edge of the strip to the inside of the hood and stitch it in place.

Next, the bodice is stitched to the pants. First, take one pants piece and cut a 1 1/2-inch slit from the waist, down the center. This will be the pants front. Refer to Figure 3-22a and align one bodice front with the notched edge of the pants front. Stitch the notched edges together and repeat, stitching the second bodice front to the pants. In the same manner, stitch the bodice back to the remaining pants piece. Press the pieces flat.

Now align these two assembled pieces. Beginning at the dot marked on the neck edge, stitch around the entire perimeter of the two pieces (Figure 3-22b).

Stitch the raw edge of the hood to the back bodice neck edge. Hem the front opening edges and the neck edge of the front bodice. Turn the suit right side out and press. Draw trapped nap out of the seams by carefully combing along the seam lines with a fine-toothed comb. Stitch four snap closures, evenly spaced, to the front edges of the suit. For ties, stitch an 8-inch length of ribbon to each lower inside edge of the hood.

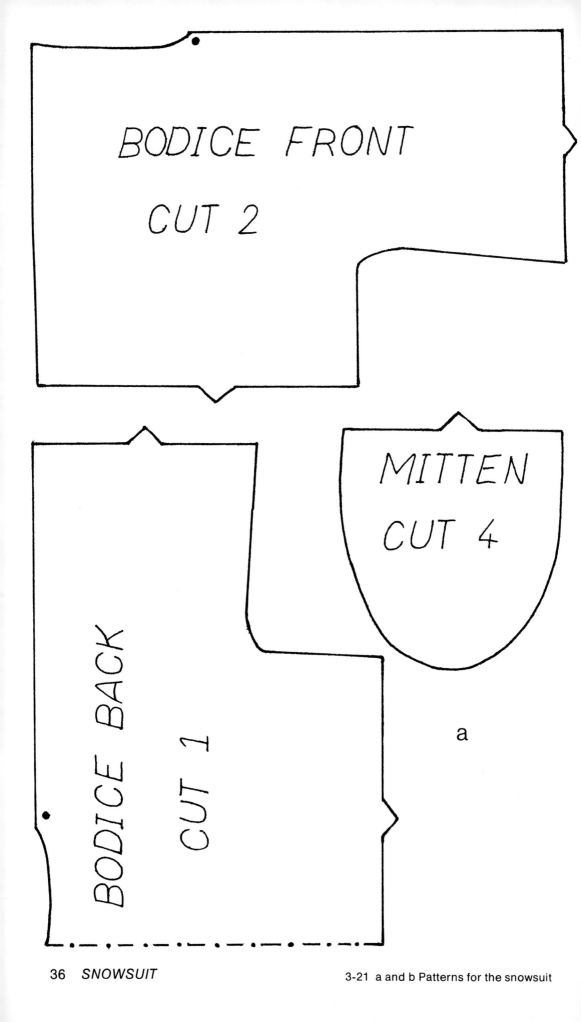

BODICE FRONT

CUT 2

MITTEN

CUT 4

BODICE BACK

CUT 1

a

3-21 a and b Patterns for the snowsuit

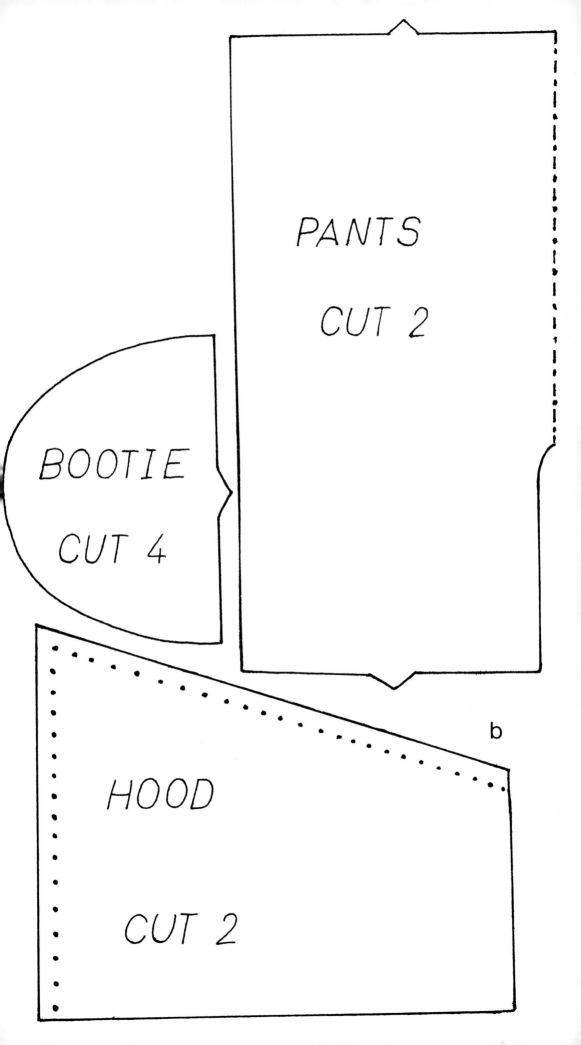

PANTS

CUT 2

BOOTIE

CUT 4

HOOD

CUT 2

b

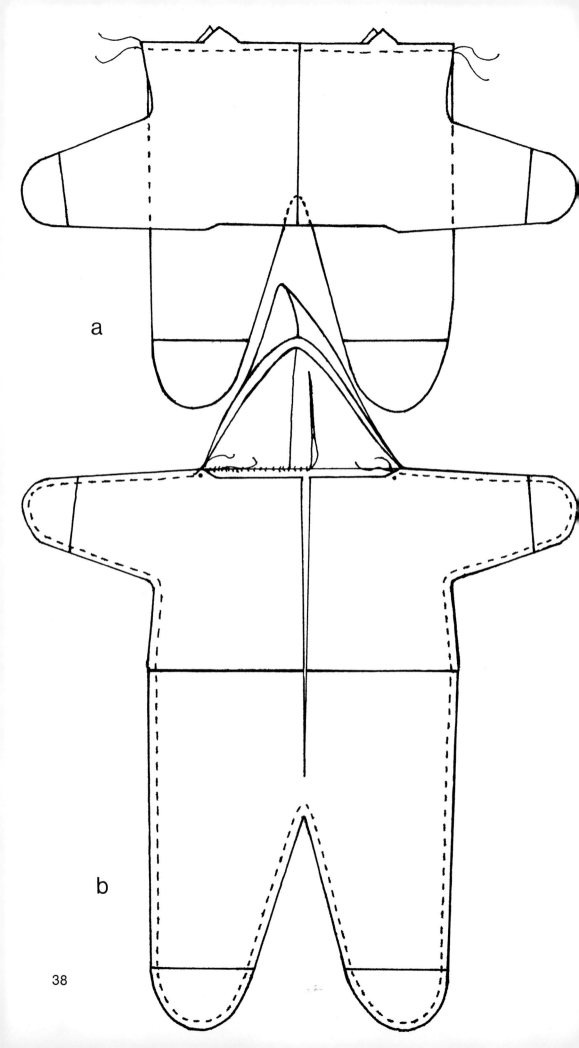

a

b

38

CHRISTENING GOWN, SLIP

The christening gown, a traditional baby garment an infant wears to church on the day it is baptized, is a lacy, beribboned affair. The pattern for the gown given here can be altered in length and used for a party dress. The gown is made of white eyelet cotton. The underslip can be constructed from any glossy fabric. I used a white fabric, but choose any color that suits your fancy.

MATERIALS

1/3 yard of eyelet cotton for the gown.
1/3 yard of glossy fabric for the underslip.
A 26-inch length of 1/2-inch-wide gathered lace
    edging to trim the gown.
1 1/2 yards of 1/4-inch-wide satin ribbon for the
    waistband and bow.
4 size 00 snaps for closures on the slip and gown.
Thread to match the fabrics.

3-23 Christening Gown
and Slip

The patterns for the gown and slip are shown in Figure 3-24. Press the gown fabric and cut one bodice front, two back pieces, and two sleeves. Cut a rectangle of fabric measuring 10 1/2 x 18 inches for the skirt. From the slip fabric cut one bodice front, two back pieces, and a rectangle of fabric measuring 9 1/4 x 17 inches for the skirt. Transfer all markings to the *wrong* side of the fabrics.

Slip. Stitch each of the back bodice pieces to the front bodice piece at the shoulder seams. Stitch the side seams from the armhole to the base of the bodice. Hem the neck edge and the armhole edges by hand or with a closely spaced machine zigzag.

Next, run a basting stitch 1/8 inch within and the length of one long edge of the slip skirt. Draw up the stitching, gathering the edge until it is the length of the waist edge of the bodice (approximately 10 3/4 inches). Align the gathered edge of the skirt with the bodice waist (Figure 3-25). The skirt should overlap the bodice by 1/2 inch. Baste and then stitch the edges together. Stitch the back seam of the skirt, from the base to within 1 1/2 inches of the waist (Figure 5-7).

Hem the back opening edges of the slip as well as the base of the skirt. Stitch two snaps to the garment, one at the neck and the second at the waist.

3-22 a. Stitching the waist of the bodice to the pants
    b. Stitching the snowsuit front to the back and
       attaching the hood

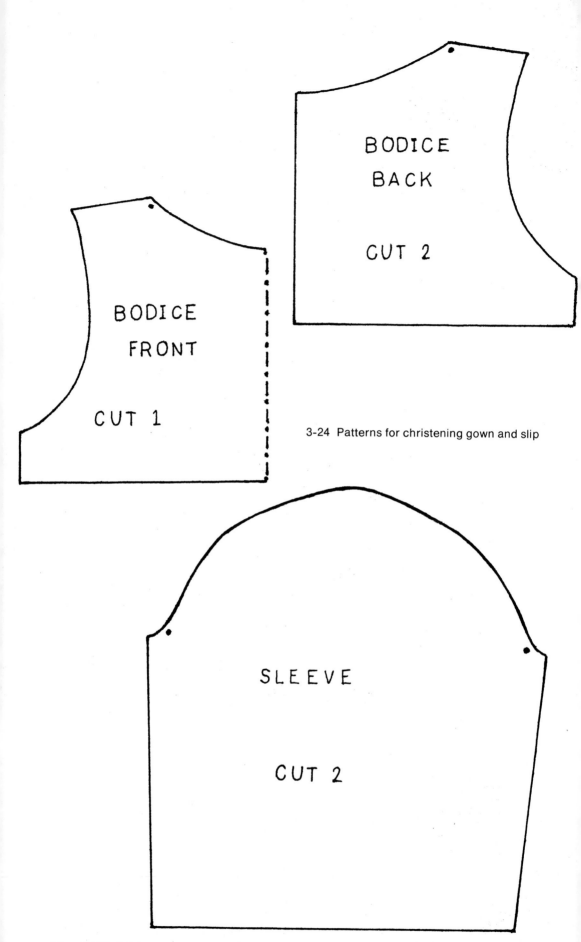

BODICE
BACK

CUT 2

BODICE
FRONT

CUT 1

3-24 Patterns for christening gown and slip

SLEEVE

CUT 2

English Riding Suit, Pants Suit, Halter Top, and Everyday Dress for the fashion doll.

Traveling Suit, Turtleneck Shirt, and Slacks for the toddler doll.

Diaper, T-Shirt, Pajamas, Sweater, Bonnet, and Booties for the baby doll.

Receiving Blanket, Hooded Towel, Bibbed Overalls, Blouse, Romper Suit, and Bonnet for the baby doll.

Gingham Dress, Apron, and Party Dress for the toddler doll.

Ballerina Costume.

Princess Costume.

Slip, Robe, Nightgown, and Slippers for
the toddler doll.

Snowsuit, Christening Gown, and Slip
for the baby doll.

Swimsuit, Tennis Outfit, Lounging Pajamas, Evening Gown, and Fur Coat for
the fashion doll.

Dress Shirt, Tie, Plaid Slacks, Pajamas, Swimsuit, and Sporty Outfit for the action doll.

Cowgirl and Indian Costumes.

Another Sporty Outfit.

Gown. With one main difference, the gown and the slip are similarly constructed: the gown has set-in sleeves. Begin the gown by stitching the two back bodice pieces to the front piece at the shoulder seams. Before inserting the sleeves refer to Figure 6-4b. Run a basting stitch 1/8 inch within the outer edge, between the dots marked on each sleeve. Draw up this stitching to gather the edge of the sleeve slightly. With right sides together, baste the gathered edge of the sleeve to the armhole edge, adjusting the gathers for a neat fit. Stitch the sleeve to the armhole. Repeat and stitch the second sleeve to the remaining armhole. Next stitch the underarm seam from the base of the bodice to the ends of the sleeves (Figure 6-4b). Hem the ends of the sleeves and the neck edge. For a collar, stitch a length of gathered lace edging (approximately 7 1/2 inches) to the neck edge. Hem the ends of the lace.

Refer back to the directions for attaching the slip skirt to the bodice, then attach the skirt to the bodice of the gown. Hem the back opening edges and the base of the skirt. Stitch lace edging around the lower edge of the skirt. Stitch two snaps, one to the neck edge and one to the waist at the back opening edges.

This ends the chapter on baby doll clothing. If you wish, you can vary the patterns. For instance, the bibbed overall can be made into a set of shorts, the christening gown into a flannel nightie, and the snowsuit into terry cloth coveralls.

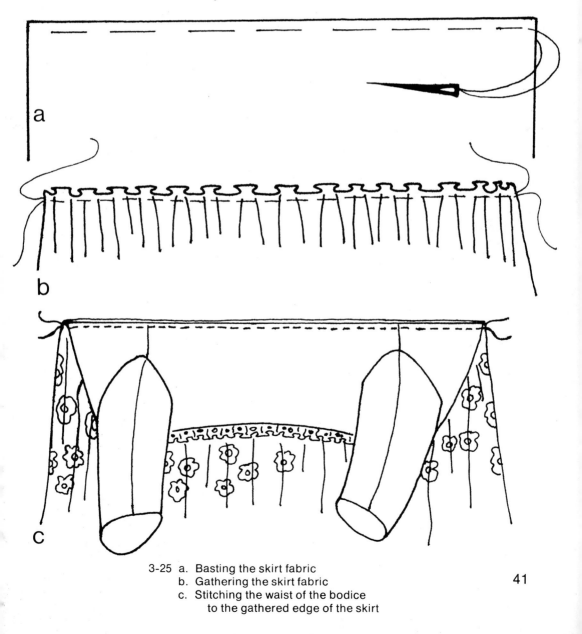

3-25 a. Basting the skirt fabric
    b. Gathering the skirt fabric
    c. Stitching the waist of the bodice
        to the gathered edge of the skirt

41

4 Clothing for the Toddler Doll

The toddler doll, first cousin to the baby doll, is a sweet-faced, cherub-limbed doll made to represent children between the ages of two and six. Young children take much pleasure dressing and undressing them, especially if the doll's clothing is pretty, nicely decorated, and similar to clothing children wear themselves. Besides their value as toys for younger children, toddler dolls make interesting costume dolls because many are manufactured with very lovely faces.

The clothing in this chapter was designed for Beth, a Madame Alexander Doll from the Little Woman series. Her measurements are: height, 12 inches; chest, 5 1/2 inches; hips, 6 1/2 inches; length of arm, 3 1/2 inches; length of inner leg, 5 inches; circumference of head, 7 1/2 inches. Measure your own doll and if its dimensions are different, make pattern adjustments as outlined in chapter 1.

SLIP AND PANTIES

Lingerie is the foundation of any wardrobe. You can choose a crisp white cotton for these garments, or any kind of silky, glossy fabrics in white or pastel colors. Printed fabrics or fabrics of a bright color will often show through the outer garment, and for this reason are usually avoided when making underclothing.

MATERIALS

1/4 yard of fabric for the slip and panties.
A 5 1/2-inch length of 1/4-inch-wide elastic.
One small snap closure.
Thread to match the fabric.

4-1 Slip

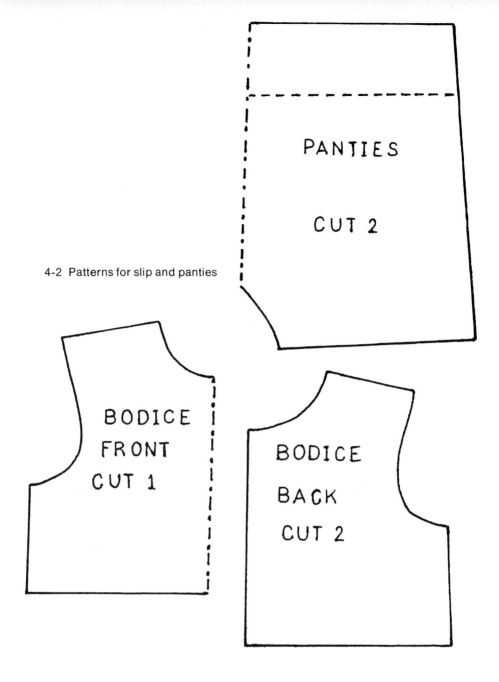

4-2 Patterns for slip and panties

PANTIES

CUT 2

BODICE
FRONT
CUT 1

BODICE

BACK

CUT 2

Cut out the patterns for the slip bodice and the panties (Figure 4-2). Use them as guides and cut the fabrics. Cut two panty pieces, two back bodice pieces and one front bodice. Cut a rectangle of fabric 4 3/4 x 15 inches for the skirt part of the slip. Transfer all markings to the wrong side of the fabric.

Panties. Take the two panty pieces and stitch *one* side seam from the waist edge to the base of the leg. Open out the piece and press it flat. Turn and press 1/4 inch of fabric along the waist edge to the inside. Stitch the edge in place. Turn and press 1/2 inch of fabric along this same edge to the inside. Stitch close to both edges of the folded piece to create a casing for the elastic (Figure 3-7). Thread the 5 1/2-inch length of elastic through the casing and stitch it to both ends of the casing. Stitch the remaining side of the panties, stitching the ends of the casing together (Figure 4-3b). Stitch the crotch seam. Hem the legs. Press the finished garment.

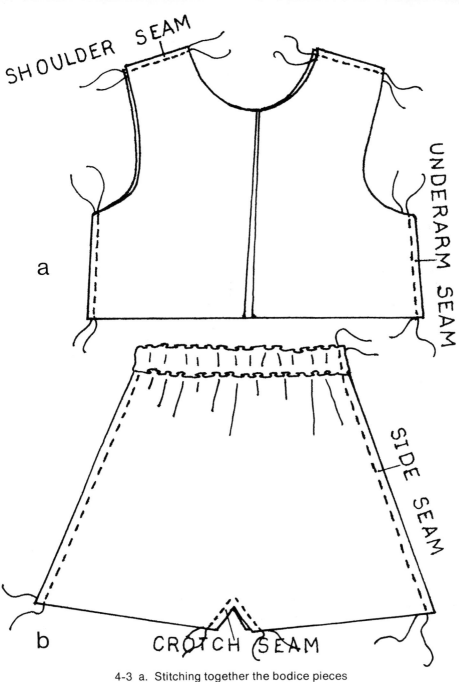

SHOULDER SEAM

UNDERARM SEAM

a

SIDE SEAM

b

CROTCH SEAM

4-3 a. Stitching together the bodice pieces
   b. Stitching together the panties

Slip. Start by stitching the two bodice back pieces to the front at the shoulder seams (Figure 4-3a). Stitch the underarm seams. Hem the neck edge, the armhole opening, and the back opening edges. Next take the rectangle of fabric you cut for the skirt of the slip and run a basting stitch the length of and close to one long edge. Draw up this stitching to gather the edge to the length of the bodice waist (approximately 7 inches). Refer to Figure 3-25 and align the waist edge of the bodice with the gathered edge of the skirt, allowing 1/2 inch of the skirt to overlap each side of the bodice. Baste and then stitch the bodice part of the skirt. Stitch the back seam of the skirt from the base to within 1 inch of the waist (Figure 5-7). Hem the lower edge of the skirt and the back opening edges (which are raw) below the waist. Turn the slip right side out and press. Stitch a snap closure to the back neck edge.

FLANNEL NIGHTGOWN, QUILTED ROBE, FURRY SLIPPERS

Nightware is important clothing for any child's doll. It sometimes eases the strain of bedtime if a favorite doll can be prepared for bed and tucked away a few minutes before the child. For the outfit pictured, use flannel for the nightgown, quilted fabric for the robe, and a scrap of imitation fur fabric for the slippers. If you are making clothing for a boy doll, choose red or plaid flannel, and omit the ruffle and the lace trimming the nightgown to make a nightshirt. The robe can be made from blue or green terry cloth with a braided yarn tie for a boy doll.

MATERIALS

1/3 yard of cotton flannel for the nightgown.
1/3 yard of quilted fabric for the robe.
A scrap of fake fur measuring approximately 2 x 6
    inches for the slippers.
A 6 1/2-inch length of 1/4-inch-wide lace edging to
    trim the nightgown.
One small snap to close the back of the nightgown.
A 21-inch length of satin ribbon for the robe tie.
An 18-inch length of bias tape to trim the neck and
    base of the robe.
A 16-inch length of embroidery thread for ties on
    the slippers.
A 4 x 5-inch piece of black felt for the soles of the
    slippers, and a piece of lightweight cardboard
    the same size for the sole inserts.
Thread to match the fabrics.

4-4 Robe, Nightgown,
    and Slippers

Using the patterns in Figure 4-5a and b as guides, cut two nightgown pieces, two robe fronts and one robe back. Cut a 2 x 20-inch piece for the nightgown ruffle. Cut two fur uppers for the slippers, two felt soles, and two cardboard soles. Transfer the X to the wrong side of *one* nightgown piece only. Transfer all other markings to the wrong side of the fabrics.

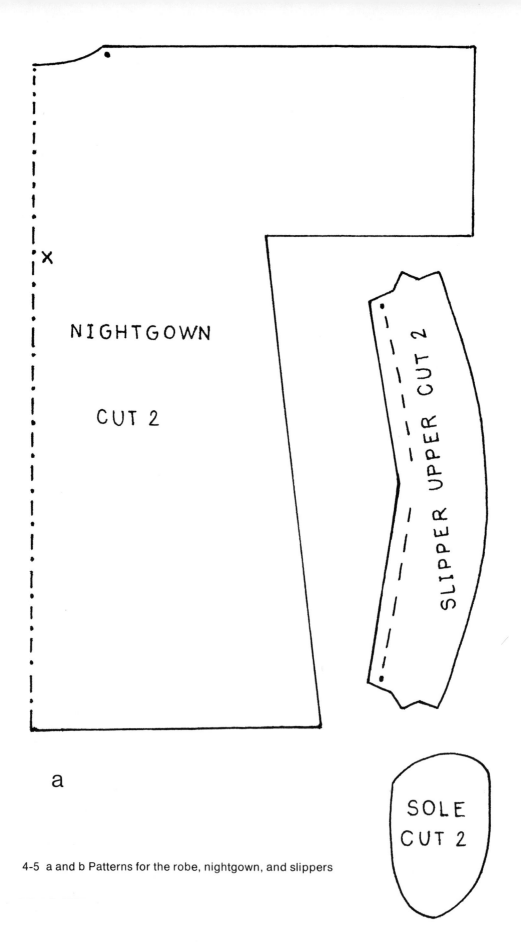

NIGHTGOWN

CUT 2

x

a

SLIPPER UPPER CUT 2

SOLE
CUT 2

4-5 a and b Patterns for the robe, nightgown, and slippers

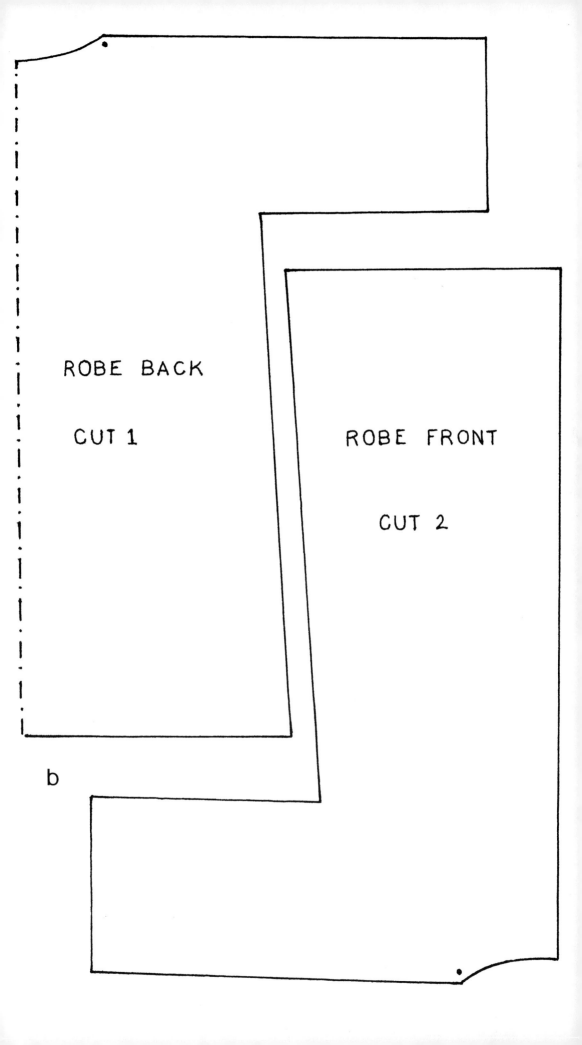

ROBE BACK

CUT 1

b

ROBE FRONT

CUT 2

Nightgown. Start with the back nightgown piece marked X. Cut a slit from the neck edge to the X. Next align the front piece with the back piece and stitch the shoulder seams from the ends of the sleeves to the dot marked on the neck edge. Stitch the underarm seams from the underside of the sleeves to the base of the gown. Hem the neck edge, the edges of the slit, and the ends of the sleeves. Stitch a narrow strip of lace edging to the neck for decoration.

To make the ruffle that trims the base of the gown, first stitch the narrow ends of the rectangular piece of fabric together so you have a hoop of fabric. Next align the raw edges and press the piece (wrong sides together) so you have a narrow hoop of fabric with two right sides. Run a basting stitch 1/8 inch within the raw edge (Figure 4-6). Draw up this stitching and gather the hoop to correspond with the length of the base of the gown (approximately 12 1/2 inches). With right sides of the fabrics together, align the raw edge of the ruffle with the base of the gown. Baste and then stitch the ruffle to the gown, arranging the ruffles so they are uniform. Stitch a snap closure to the neck edge of the nightgown. Press.

Robe. The robe is made from quilted fabric. Take the three robe pieces (two front pieces and one back piece) and stitch each of the front pieces to the back piece at the shoulder seams which extend

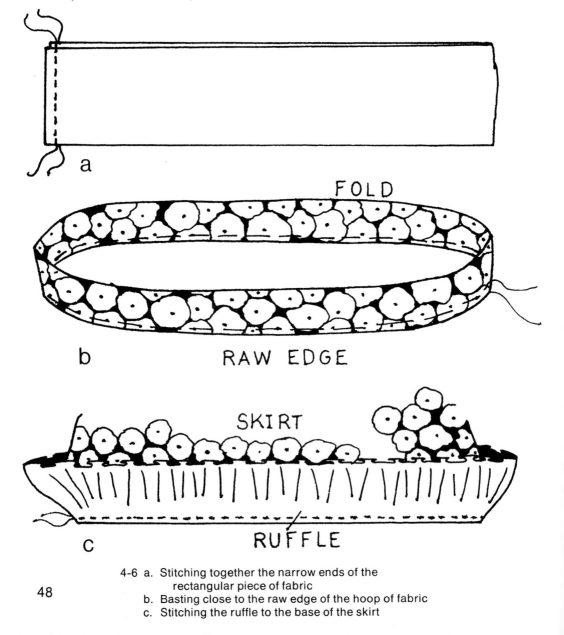

FOLD

RAW EDGE

SKIRT

RUFFLE

4-6 a. Stitching together the narrow ends of the
rectangular piece of fabric
b. Basting close to the raw edge of the hoop of fabric
c. Stitching the ruffle to the base of the skirt

from the neck edge to the ends of the sleeves (Figure 3-3). Next stitch the underarm seams. Hem the front opening edges and the base of the sleeves. To finish the neck edge and the base of the robe, use a matching or contrasting color of bias tape and bind off these edges. This procedure is illustrated in Figure 4-7 and explained in detail in chapter 6. Now stitch a loop of embroidery thread at waist level on each underarm seam to carry the satin ribbon belt. Press and the robe is done.

Slippers. Begin by trimming 1/8 inch from the perimeter of each cardboard sole. Glue the cardboard to the felt sole, making sure you have both a left and a right sole (Figure 6-6a). Zigzag stitch or edge stitch between the dots, close to each curved edge of the fur uppers. Stitch together the notched ends of the uppers. Trim off the notches. Open out the unstitched base of each upper and fit a felt sole (with the cardboard sole inside) into the opening. Overcast stitch the edge of a felt sole to the edge of each upper (Figure 6-6d). Thread a length of embroidery thread in and out through the slashes marked on the fur fabric. Put the slippers on the doll and draw up the embroidery thread so the slippers fit accurately but can still be slipped on and off. Tie a bow over the toe of each slipper.

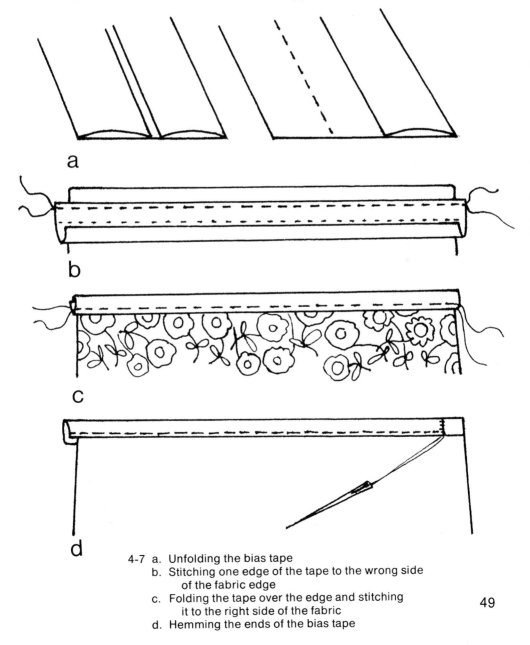

a

b

c

d

4-7 a. Unfolding the bias tape
b. Stitching one edge of the tape to the wrong side
of the fabric edge
c. Folding the tape over the edge and stitching
it to the right side of the fabric
d. Hemming the ends of the bias tape

49

SLACKS OR SHORTS, KNIT TURTLENECK SHIRT

This sporty outfit consists of flare-legged pants and a long-sleeved turtleneck shirt. The slacks can be made into shorts by simply cutting the pattern at the solid line marked for this purpose. The turtleneck shirt is also versatile. It can be made in a variety of colors with long or short sleeves. Knit fabrics are recommended for the shirt.

MATERIALS

1/4 yard of fabric for the slacks or shorts.
1/4 yard knit fabric for the shirt.
Two small snap closures (size 00).
Thread to match the fabrics.

4-8 Slacks and
Turtleneck Shirt

Cut two shirt pieces, two slacks pieces (Figure 4-9), one rectangle of slacks fabric measuring 1 1/2 x 7 inches for the waistband, and a rectangle of shirt fabric measuring 2 1/4 x 6 inches for the turtleneck. Transfer the X marked on the shirt pattern to the wrong side of *one* shirt piece only. Transfer all other markings to the wrong side of the fabrics.

Slacks or Shorts. Align the two pieces and stitch *one* side seam from the base of the leg to the waist edge. Stitch the second side seam from the base of the leg, but end the stitching at the dot marked on the fabric. Next stitch the entire crotch seam from the base of one leg around to the base of the second leg. Hem the base of the legs and narrowly hem (1/4 inch) the edge of the opening in the one side.

With right sides together, fold the strip of fabric for the waistband in half, so you have a long narrow piece. Stitch the narrow ends together (Figure 4-10a). Turn the piece right side out and press. Align the raw edge of the waistband with the raw edge of the waist (Figure 4-10b). The ends of the waistband should overlap the opening in the side of the slacks by 1/4 inch. Baste and then stitch the waistband to the waist. Press the waistband up. Stitch a snap closure to the over-lapping ends of the band. Press the slacks, creasing them if you want.

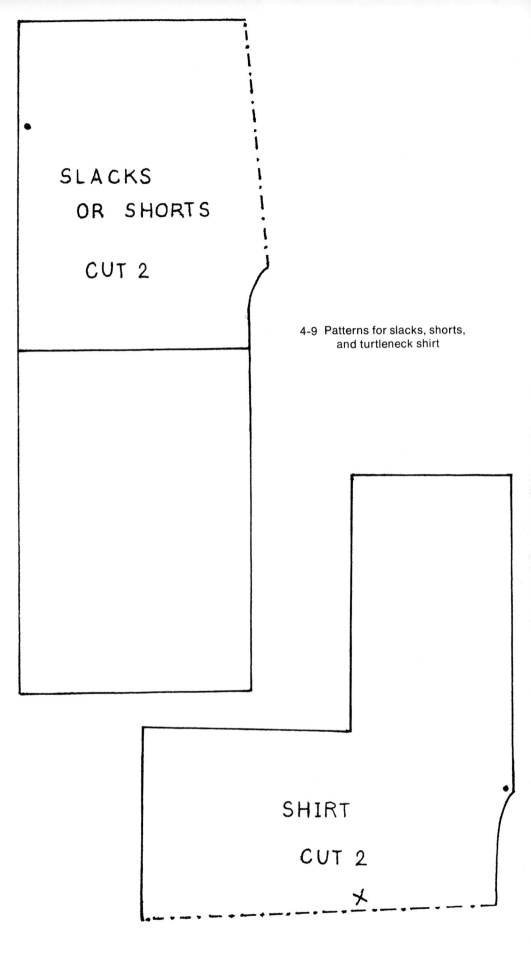

SLACKS
OR SHORTS

CUT 2

4-9 Patterns for slacks, shorts, and turtleneck shirt

SHIRT

CUT 2

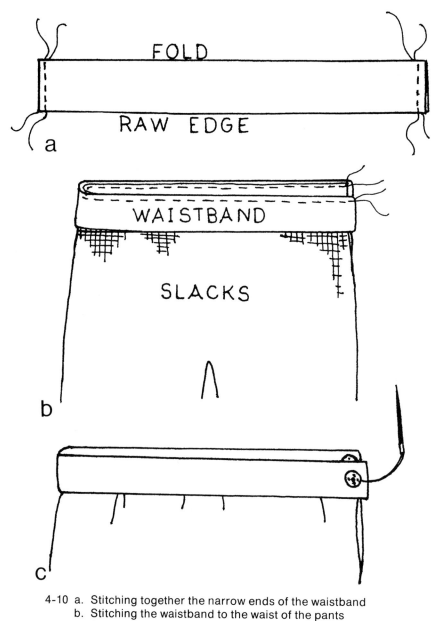

4-10 a. Stitching together the narrow ends of the waistband
b. Stitching the waistband to the waist of the pants
c. Stitching snaps to the waistband

Shirt. The shirt is constructed from three pieces: front, back, and a neck strip. Start with the shirt back, marked with an X. Cut a slit from the neck edge to the X. Next align the shirt front and back, and stitch the shoulder seams from the dot marked at the neck edge to the ends of the sleeves. Stitch the underarm seams from the tips of the sleeves to the base of the blouse. Narrowly hem the edges of the slit. To make the turtleneck collar, fold the strip of knit fabric in half as you did for the waistband. You have a long narrow piece. Stitch the short ends together (Figure 4-10a). Turn the strip right side out and press. Baste the raw edges of the strip (right sides together) to the raw edge of the neck of the shirt. Align the ends of the strip with the back opening edges of the shirt. Stitch the strip to the shirt. Press it up, creating the turtleneck. Stitch a snap closure to the ends of the strip. Hem the ends of the sleeves and the base of the shirt. Press.

TRAVELING SUIT

The traveling suit consists of a matching plaid gathered skirt and blazer jacket, topped off with a white felt hat. The turtleneck in the previous section is worn beneath the jacket. If you prefer a pants suit, substitute slacks for the skirt.

MATERIALS

1/4 yard of fabric for the skirt and jacket.
A 5 1/2-inch length of 1/4-inch-wide elastic.
A 5 x 7-inch rectangle of felt for the hat and pockets.
An 11-inch length of 1/2-inch-wide gathered lace edging for the hat brim.
One small snap closure.
Thread to match the fabrics.

4-11 Traveling Suit

Figure 4-12 shows the patterns for the jacket front, jacket back, and the hat. Cut one jacket back and two front pieces. Cut two strips of jacket fabric measuring 1 1/2 x 5 inches for the front facings. From felt cut two hat pieces, a strip measuring 1 1/2 x 4 inches for the hat gusset, and a strip measuring 1/4 x 4 inches for the hat strap. Also from felt cut two rectangles measuring 1 x 1 1/4 inches for the jacket pockets. Cut a rectangle of fabric measuring 12 1/2 x 5 1/2 inches for the skirt. Transfer the slashes and dots on the jacket front pattern to the right side of the fabric. Transfer all other markings to the wrong side of the fabric.

Skirt. The skirt is very easy to assemble. Turn, press, and stitch 1/4 inch of fabric along one long edge to the inside. Turn an additional 1/2 inch of fabric along the same edge to the inside. Stitch close to both edges of this folded piece to create a casing for the elastic (Figure 3-7). Thread the elastic through the casing, then stitch it to each end of the casing. Stitch together the two narrow ends of the skirt, closing the ends of the casing as you do so. Hem the base of the skirt. Press and the skirt is finished.

Jacket. Begin by stitching the front to the back at the shoulder seams. Stitch the underarm seams (Figure 3-3). The front facings consist of two strips of fabric. Refer to Figure 4-13 and with right sides together, align and stitch one facing to each front opening

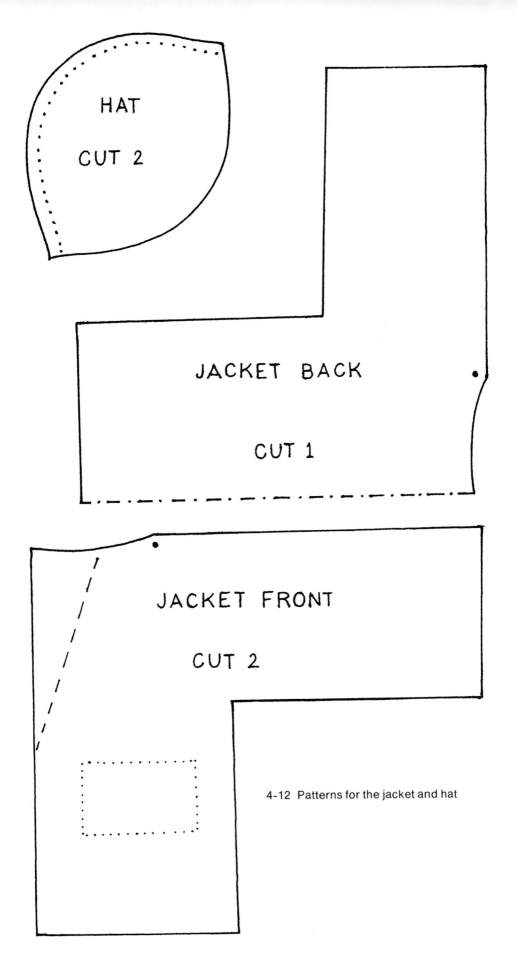

HAT

CUT 2

JACKET BACK

CUT 1

JACKET FRONT

CUT 2

4-12 Patterns for the jacket and hat

edge. Turn the facings to the inside and press in place. Next hem the neck edge, the ends of the sleeves, and the base of the jacket. Stitch a pocket to each side of the lower jacket front, over the dots marked to aid placement. You can do this by machine or hand. To create lapels, fold back the upper front opening edges, along the marked slashes, exposing the facing. Press, and tack the lapels in place with a few concealed stitches.

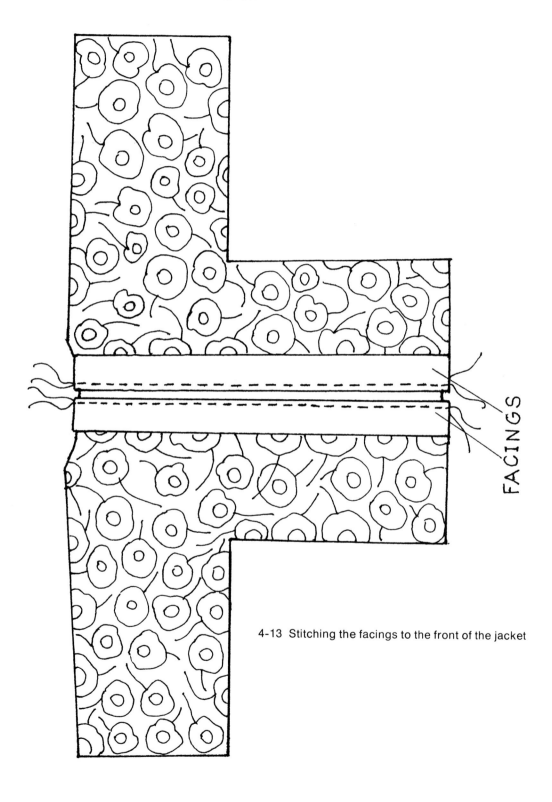

FACINGS

4-13 Stitching the facings to the front of the jacket

Hat. The hat is constructed from two side pieces and a gusset to give it shape. Align one long edge of the gusset with the edge of the hat marked with a dotted stitching line (Figure 3-19a). Baste and then stitch the gusset to the hat piece. Stitch the second side of the gusset to the dotted edge of the remaining side piece. Edgestitch the short edge of one end of the gusset (this will be the back of the hat). For a brim, stitch the length of narrow lace edging along the unstitched edge of the sides of the hat and gusset. Next edgestitch along all edges of the piece you cut for the hat strap. Stitch one end of the strap to one point marked X on the inside of the hat. Stitch 1/2 of a snap closure to the opposite end of the strap. Stitch the remaining half of the snap to the other X marked on the hat.

GINGHAM DRESS, APRON

The dress described here does not necessarily have to be made from gingham, but gingham looks so fresh, crisp, and sprightly on a doll, especially when highlighted by a white apron, that I recommend it. If you omit the lace trimming the armholes, the dress can second as a jumper. The turtleneck shirt can serve as an underblouse. The apron is made from white eyelet cotton with lace edging and satin ribbon ties.

MATERIALS

1/4 yard of fabric for the dress.
A 21-inch length of 1/2-inch-wide lace edging to
  trim the dress and the apron.
1/8 yard of fabric for the apron.
A 21-inch length of 1/4-inch-wide satin ribbon for
  the apron strings.
One small snap closure.
Thread to match the fabrics.

4-14 Gingham Dress and Apron

Cut one bodice front, two bodice back pieces, and two apron pieces (Figure 4-15). Cut a rectangle of fabric measuring 5 x 15 inches for the skirt. Transfer all markings to the wrong side of the fabrics.

Dress. Start by stitching the two bodice back pieces to the front bodice piece at the shoulder seams (Figure 4-3a). Stitch the under-arm seams to the waist. Hem the armhole openings, the neck edge, and the back opening edges. Stitch a 5-inch length of lace edging to

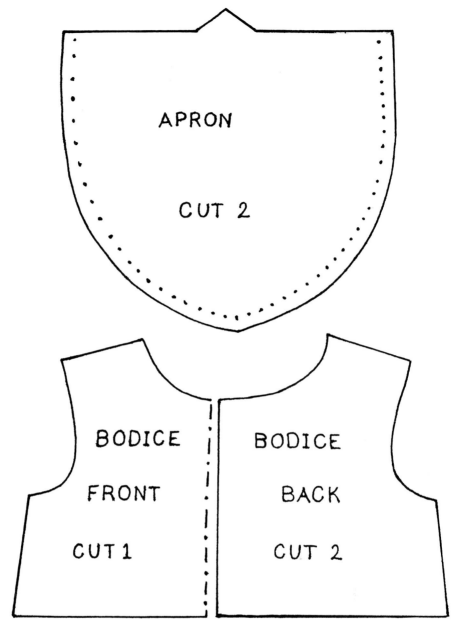

APRON

CUT 2

BODICE FRONT CUT 1

BODICE BACK CUT 2

4-15 Patterns for gingham dress and apron

each armhole opening. Begin to stitch the lace strip 1/4 inch beyond the underarm seam. Stitch the lace over the shoulder and end the stitching 1/4 inch before you reach the underarm seam. Do not stitch the ends of the lace together, but hem each end.

Now gather the rectangular piece of skirt fabric and run a basting stitch close to and the length of one long edge. Draw up the stitching so the fabric is gathered to match the length of the bodice waist (approximately 6 3/4 inches). Align the raw gathered edge of the skirt with the bodice waist (Figure 3-25). The skirt should overlap the back opening edges of the bodice by 1/2 inch. Baste and stitch the skirt to the bodice. Stitch together the raw edges of the back of the skirt, from the base of the skirt to within 1 inch of the bodice waist (Figure 5-7). Hem the remaining raw edges to the point where they join the bodice. Hem the base of the skirt. Press the dress. Stitch a snap closure to the bodice neck at the back, and stitch a second snap below the first, at the waist.

Apron. Stitch the two apron pieces to one another, stitching over the dotted stitching lines marked on the fabric (Figure 4-16). Turn the piece right side out. Turn and press 1/4 inch of each upper raw edge to the inside. Stitch the upper edges together. Stitch a piece of gathered lace edging to the curved edge of the apron, hemming the ends of the lace. For a waistband and tie, stitch the satin ribbon to the straight upper edge of the apron.

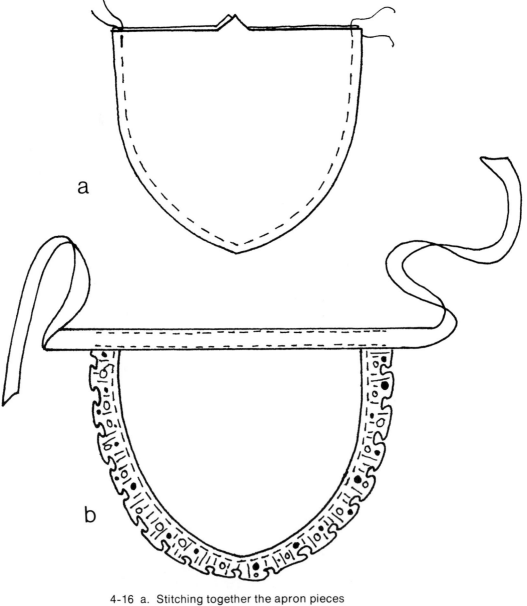

4-16 a. Stitching together the apron pieces
b. Stitching lace and ribbon to the apron

PARTY DRESS

The party dress pictured here is made of dotted swiss, trimmed with pink rickrack and blue satin ribbon. Any of a variety of fabrics such as lace, eyelet cotton, chiffon, or velvet would be equally as festive. Trims of rhinestones, sequins, or beads could also be used.

MATERIALS

1/4 yard of fabric for the dress.
Two pieces of 1/4-inch-wide elastic, each 3 1/2
   inches in length.
An 18-inch length of satin ribbon for the waistband.
A 38-inch length of 1/2-inch-wide rickrack.
Two small snap closures.
Thread to match the fabrics.

4-17 Party Dress

You will find the patterns for the party dress in Figure 4-18. Cut one bodice front, two bodice back pieces, two sleeves, two collars, and a rectangle of fabric measuring 5 x 17 1/2 inches for the skirt. Transfer the dotted lines on the bodice front to the right side of the fabric. Transfer all other markings to the wrong side of the fabric.

Bodice and Sleeves. Begin by assembling the bodice pieces, stitching the back bodice piece to the front bodice piece along the shoulder seams. Next hem the back opening edges. Refer to Figure 6-4b which illustrates sleeve insertion. Run a line of basting stitches between the dots marked on the curved edge of each sleeve. Slightly draw up this stitching to gather the sleeve. With right sides together, align the gathered edge of the sleeve with the armhole opening. Adjust the gathers so the sleeve fits accurately into the armhole. Baste and then stitch each sleeve to the armholes.

Casing. To elasticize the sleeves and give them a bubble effect it is necessary to make casings. Fold, press, and stitch 1/4 inch of the end of each sleeve to the inside. Fold and press an additional 1/2 inch of fabric along each sleeve end to the inside. To create a casing, stitch close to both edges of this folded piece (Figure 3-7). Thread a 3 1/2-inch length of 1/4-inch-wide elastic through each casing. Stitch

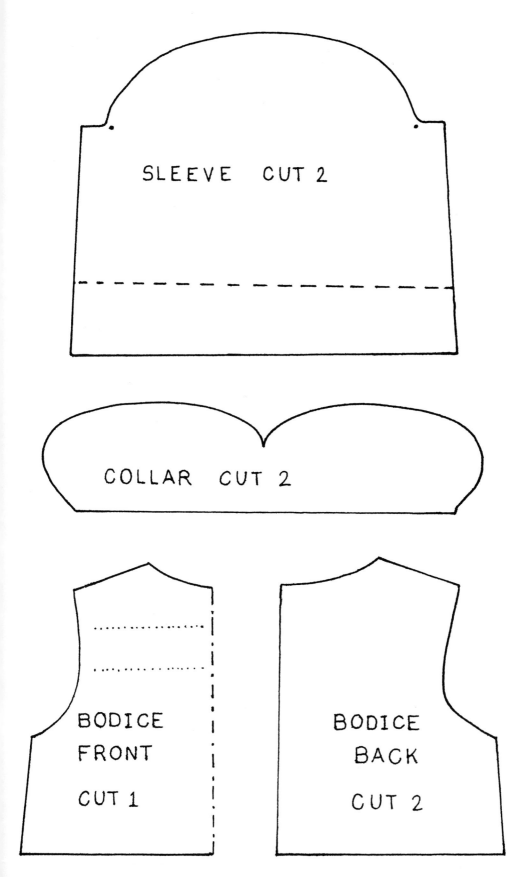

4-18 Patterns for the party dress

the elastic to each end of the casing. Stitch the underarm seams of the bodice. Stitch from the waist to the ends of the sleeves, stitching the casings together as you proceed.

Collar. Begin the collar by pressing 1/4 inch of the notched edge of *one* collar piece to the inside. Align the second collar piece over the first. Stitch the curved edge of the pair together. Refer to Figure 3-16 before continuing. This diagram illustrates basic collar attachment. With right sides together, align the unfolded edge of the collar with the inside neck edge of the dress. Baste and then stitch these edges together. Press the seam toward the collar, then turn the folded edge of the collar to the outside over the seam. Stitch this edge in place by hand. Topstitch the curved edge of the collar.

To attach the skirt to the bodice, gather one long edge of the rectangular skirt fabric and stitch this gathered edge to the bodice waist, with 1/2 inch of the skirt fabric overlapping the ends of the bodice to allow for a seam (Figure 3-25). Stitch together the back of the skirt, from the base to within 1 inch of the waist (Figure 5-7). Hem the edges of the opening below the waist. Also hem the base of the skirt. Press the dress and stitch a snap closure to the neck edge, and another closure to the waist at the back opening. To finish the dress, stitch two rows of rickrack around the base of the skirt. Stitch a length of rickrack over each dotted line marked on the bodice front.

As you can see, all of the patterns are versatile and can be changed in a number of ways to make new and different garments. To add even more interest to a doll's wardrobe you can make accessories by topstitching two layers of felt together with a thin wad of stuffing between the pieces, creating handbags, suitcases, baskets of flowers, and so on.

5 Outfits for Fashion and Action Dolls

Making their appearance within the last twenty years, fashion and action dolls are latecomers to the world of toy dolls. Representing long-legged shapely women or muscular ruggedly handsome men, these dolls hold special significance for preteens who are developing notions of the glamour, romance, and adventure of the adult. For this reason the dolls require a different kind of clothing: evening gowns, fur coats, sporty suits, and formal attire.

The fashion doll patterns in the first part of this chapter were designed for Mattel's Barbie Doll. Her measurements are: height, 11 inches; chest, 5 1/2 inches; hips, 5 inches; waist, 3 1/2 inches; length of arm, 3 1/2 inches; length of inner leg, 4 inches. Again, compare the measurements of your doll, and alter patterns if necessary.

SWIMSUIT

The clothes for these dolls are relatively small and you will find it necessary to do more hand sewing than for the previous outfits. Also, 1/2-inch hems tend to be too bulky for the small garments, so I suggest you use 1/4-inch hems whenever possible. This swimsuit, for example, can be easily and neatly stitched by hand. The pattern has no darts, because of the doll's shapely figure. It is necessary to cut the swimsuit from a stretchable knit fabric.

MATERIALS

A scrap of knit fabric measuring 5 x 8 inches for
  the swimsuit.
Two small snap closures.
Thread to match the fabrics.

5-1 Swimsuit

Using the pattern shown in Figure 5-2, cut two swimsuit pieces. Transfer all markings to the *wrong* side of the fabric.

With right sides together, align the two swimsuit pieces. Using the dotted lines as guides, stitch the side seams and the crotch seam. Next narrowly hem the leg openings, the armholes, the ends of the straps, and the neck edge. To finish the swimsuit, stitch a snap closure to each pair of shoulder straps (Figure 5-3). Press.

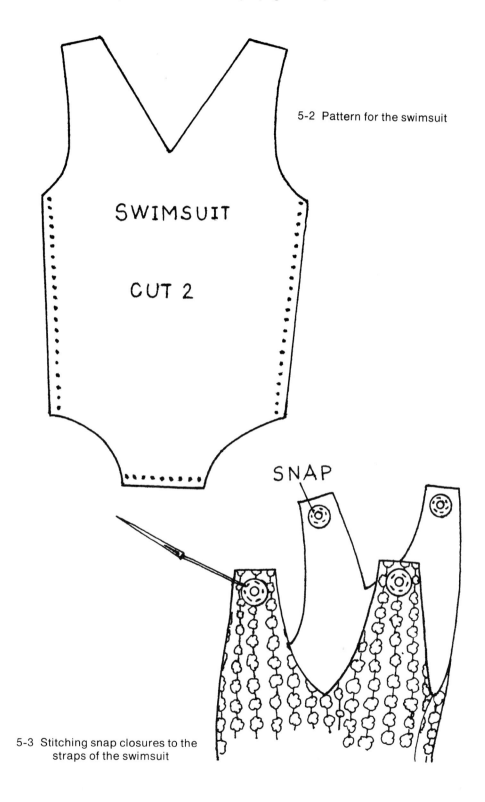

5-2 Pattern for the swimsuit

SWIMSUIT

CUT 2

SNAP

5-3 Stitching snap closures to the straps of the swimsuit

TENNIS OUTFIT

The tennis outfit is made from ribbed white cotton. The dress has matching shorts. The pattern can also be used to make lingerie; just substitute silky, pliable fabric and you will have a slip and panties.

MATERIALS

1/8 yard of fabric for the dress and shorts.
A 7-inch length of bias tape to bind the back open-
    ing edges (optional).
A 4 1/2-inch length of 1/8-inch-wide elastic.
Two small snap closures.
Thread to match the fabrics.

Using the patterns shown in Figure 5-5, cut one bodice front, two bodice backs. Cut two shorts pieces. Cut a rectangle of fabric measuring 3 x 12 inches for the skirt. Transfer all markings to the wrong side of the fabric.

5-4 Tennis Outfit

Shorts. Align the two shorts pieces. Stitch *one* side seam from the waist to the base of the leg. Open out the piece and press it flat. Turn, press, and stitch 1/4 inch of fabric along the waist edge to the inside. Turn and press an additional 1/4 inch of fabric along this same edge to the inside. Stitch close to both edges of the folded piece, creating a casing for the elastic (Figure 3-7). Thread a 4 1/2-inch length of elastic through the casing and stitch it to each end of the casing. Stitch the second side seam of the shorts, stitching together the ends of the casing as you proceed (Figure 4-3b). Stitch the crotch seam. Hem the base of the legs. Press the completed shorts.

Dress. Begin the dress with the bodice. There are two darts marked on the bodice front. Fold and stitch the darts (Figure 5-6). Press the darts down. Align the front of the bodice with each back piece (Figure 4-3a). Stitch the shoulder seams and the underarm seams. Narrowly hem the neck edge and the armholes.
Gather the rectangular piece of fabric for the skirt by running a

basting stitch the length of the piece and 1/8 inch within the outer edge. Draw up the stitching and gather the edge to match the length of the bodice waist (approximately 4 3/4 inches). Align the gathered edge of the skirt with the bodice waist edge (Figure 3-25). Baste and then stitch the edges together. Press the seam toward the bodice. Topstitch close to the point where the bodice joins the skirt. Next, stitch the back seam of the skirt, beginning stitching at the base and ending 1 inch below the waist (Figure 5-7).

The back opening edges of the dress can be hemmed, or bind them with a matching or contrasting color of bias tape. This procedure is illustrated in Figure 4-7. Hem the base of the skirt. Stitch a snap closure to the neck and waist of the back opening edges. Press.

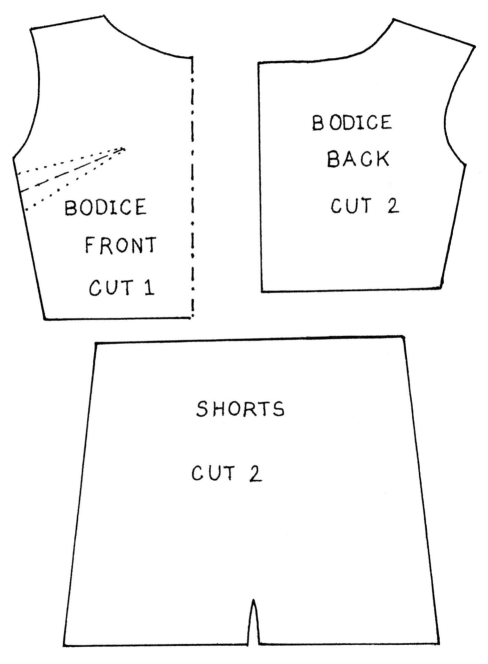

5-5 Patterns for the tennis outfit

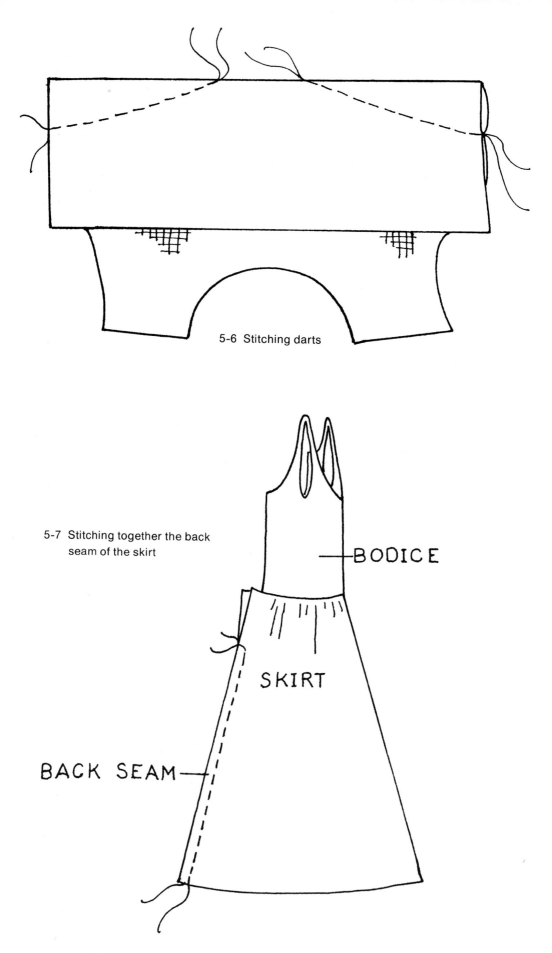

5-6 Stitching darts

5-7 Stitching together the back seam of the skirt

BODICE

SKIRT

BACK SEAM

LOUNGING PAJAMAS

Like the swimsuit, these slinky pajamas are made from knit fabric. Knits accurately fit a fashion doll's curvaceous figure.

MATERIALS

1/8 yard of knit fabric for the pajamas.
1 yard of yarn.
Two small snap closures.
Thread to match the fabric.

5-8 Lounging Pajamas

PAJAMA

CUT 2

Using the pattern in Figure 5-9 as a guide, cut two pajama pieces. With right sides together, stitch the side seams and the crotch seam of the pajama pieces. Narrowly hem the armholes, the ends of the shoulder straps, the neck edges, and the base of the legs. Turn right side out. Press, and stitch a snap closure to each pair of straps (Figure 5-3). Press.

Braid together, knotting the ends of the braid, three 12-inch lengths of yarn to tie around the waist of the pajamas. Stitch a loop of thread to each side seam at waist level to hold the belt in place.

5-9 Pattern for lounging pajamas

PANTS SUIT, HALTER TOP

The jacket and pants which make up this outfit are cut from polished cotton. The halter is a stretchable knit tube which snaps together at the doll's back.

MATERIALS

1/8 yard of fabric for the jacket and pants.
A piece of knit fabric 2 x 4 1/2 inches for
  the halter.
Three small snap closures.
Thread to match the fabrics.

5-10 Pants Suit and Halter Top

The patterns for the jacket and pants can be seen in Figure 5-11. Cut the appropriate number of pieces marked on each pattern. Cut a rectangle of knit fabric measuring 2 x 4 1/2 inches for the halter. Transfer all markings to the wrong side of the fabric.

Halter. The halter top can be quickly and easily assembled. Fold the rectangle of fabric in half (right sides together) so you have a long narrow piece. Stitch the long raw edges opposite the fold together (Figure 5-12). Stitch together one short end. Turn the tube right side out and press. Turn 1/4 inch of fabric along each edge of the remaining short end to the inside. Stitch the folded edges together. Stitch a snap closure to the upper and lower corners, so the halter will overlap slightly in the back, fit snugly, and snap together.

Jacket. Align the jacket front pieces with the jacket back piece and stitch the shoulder seams from the tips of the sleeves to the dots marked at the neck (Figure 3-3). Stitch the underarm seams from the underside of the sleeves to the base of the jacket. Hem the neck edge, the ends of the sleeves, the front opening edges, and the base of the jacket. Press.

Pants. The pants are also very easy to assemble. Align the pants pieces. Stitch *one* side seam from the base of the leg to the waist. Stitch the second side seam from the base of the leg, but end stitching 3/4 inch below the waist. Hem the raw edges of this slit. Stitch the crotch seam, stitching from the base of one inner leg around to the base of the second leg. Hem the waist edge and the base of the legs. To hold the opening in the side closed, stitch a snap closure to the waist. Press and the pants suit is complete.

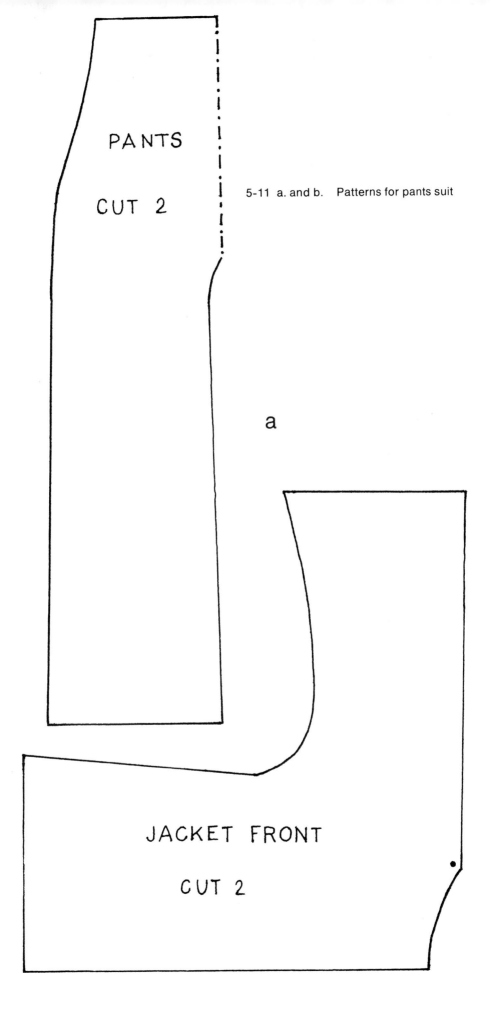

PANTS

CUT 2

5-11 a. and b.   Patterns for pants suit

a

JACKET FRONT

CUT 2

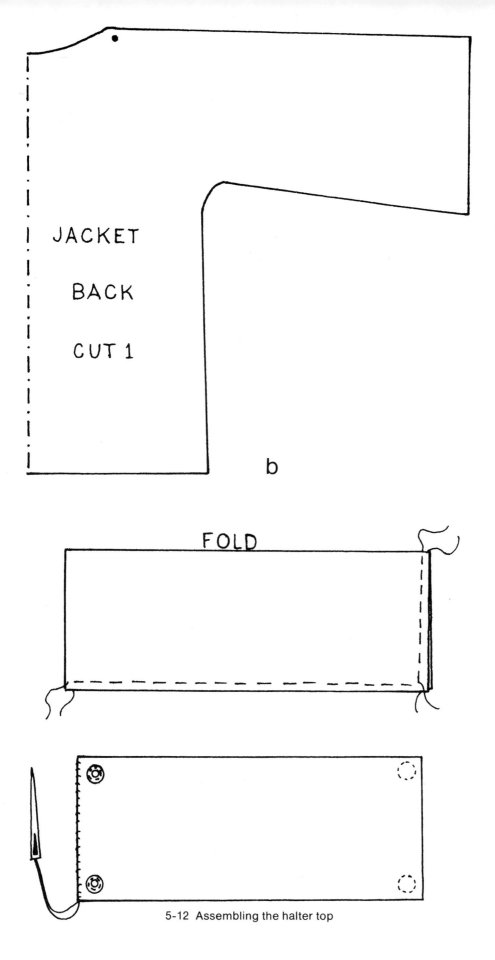

JACKET

BACK

CUT 1

b

FOLD

5-12 Assembling the halter top

EVERYDAY DRESS

The everyday dress is made from brightly printed cotton. The sleeves are set in. A satin ribbon trims the waist and lace trims the neckline and cuffs.

MATERIALS

1/8 yard of fabric for the dress.
A 12-inch length of 1/4-inch-wide gathered lace
    edging.
A 15-inch length of 1/4-inch-wide satin ribbon for
    the waistband.
Two small snap closures.
Thread to match the fabrics.

5-13 Everyday Dress

Figure 5-14 shows the patterns for the bodice and sleeves of the everyday dress. Cut one bodice front, two bodice back pieces, two sleeves, and a rectangle of fabric measuring 4 1/2 x 10 1/2 inches for the skirt. Transfer all markings to the wrong side of the fabric.

Dress. Begin the dress by stitching the two darts marked on the bodice front. Press the darts down. Then, stitch the bodice front to the two back pieces along the shoulder seams (Figure 4-3a).

To insert the sleeves, refer to Figure 6-4b which illustrates this procedure. Begin by running a basting stitch between the dots marked on the curved edge of each sleeve. Align the right side of the curved edge of the sleeve with the right side of the armhole edge. Draw up the basting stitching to ease the sleeve to fit the armhole. Baste and then stitch each sleeve to an armhole. Stitch the underarm seam from the tips of the sleeve to the base of the bodice. Hem the ends of the sleeves, the neck edge, and the back opening edges. For decoration, stitch a strip of narrow lace edging along the neck edge and around the end of each sleeve.

To attach the skirt to the dress, begin by running a basting stitch the length and 1/8 inch within one long edge of the rectangular piece of fabric you cut for the skirt. Draw up this stitching to gather the edge to the length of the bodice waist (approximately 5 inches). Align the gathered edge of the skirt with the bodice waist, 1/4 inch of skirt fabric overlapping each back opening edge of the bodice (Figure 3-25).

   Stitch the skirt to the bodice. Next stitch the back seam of the skirt from the base, ending the stitching 3/4 inch below the bodice waist (Figure 5-7). Hem the raw edges below the waist. Hem the base of the skirt. Stitch three snap closures, evenly spaced apart, to the back opening edges. To finish, arrange the ribbon waistband around the dress. Tack the ribbon to the underarm seams with a few hand stitches. Press the finished dress.

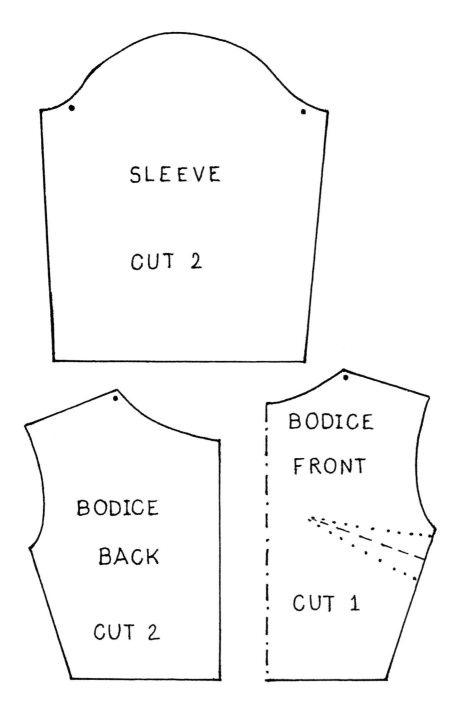

5-14 Patterns for the everyday dress

ENGLISH RIDING SUIT

The English riding suit consists of jodhpur pants, a velour blouse, and a felt vest.

MATERIALS

1/8 yard of fabric for the jodhpur pants.

1/8 yard of fabric for the blouse.

A piece of felt measuring at least 4 x 8 inches for the vest.

A strip of bias tape measuring 5 1/2 inches long by 1/2 inch wide.

Four small snap closures.

Thread to match the fabrics.

5-15 English Riding Suit

Figure 5-16 shows the patterns for the English riding suit. Cut the appropriate number of pieces as indicated on the patterns. Transfer the dotted lines marked on the jodhpur pants to the *right* side of the fabric. Transfer all other markings to the *wrong* side of the fabrics.

Jodhpur Pants. Align the two pants pieces. Stitch *one* side seam from the base of the trouser leg to the waist. Stitch the second side seam from the base of the leg to within 1/2 inch of the waist. Hem the remaining edges of the 1/2-inch opening in the side. Next stitch the crotch seam. Hem the base of the legs. Hem the waist edge. To decorate the pants, use a contrasting or matching color of thread and topstitch over the dotted lines encircling the waist and the base of the legs. Press.

Blouse. Begin by aligning the two front blouse pieces with the back piece. Stitch the shoulder and underarm seams (Figure 3-3). Hem the front opening edges, the ends of the sleeves, and the base of the blouse. To simulate a collar, bind off the neck edge with a bright color of bias tape. This procedure is illustrated in Figure 4-7 and explained in detail in chapter 6 in the section describing binding the neck edge of the princess gown. To finish the blouse stitch a snap closure to the front of the neck opening edges. Stitch a second and third snap, spaced 1/2 inch apart (small buttons and hand-worked buttonholes can replace the snaps). Press.

Vest. The vest is made from felt, a pressed rather than a woven fabric: felt edges do not fray and need not be hemmed. Stitch together the back and front vest pieces along the shoulder and underarm seams. Topstitch close to all remaining edges with a machine zigzag stitch, or by hand using an over-the-edge stitch. Press the vest.

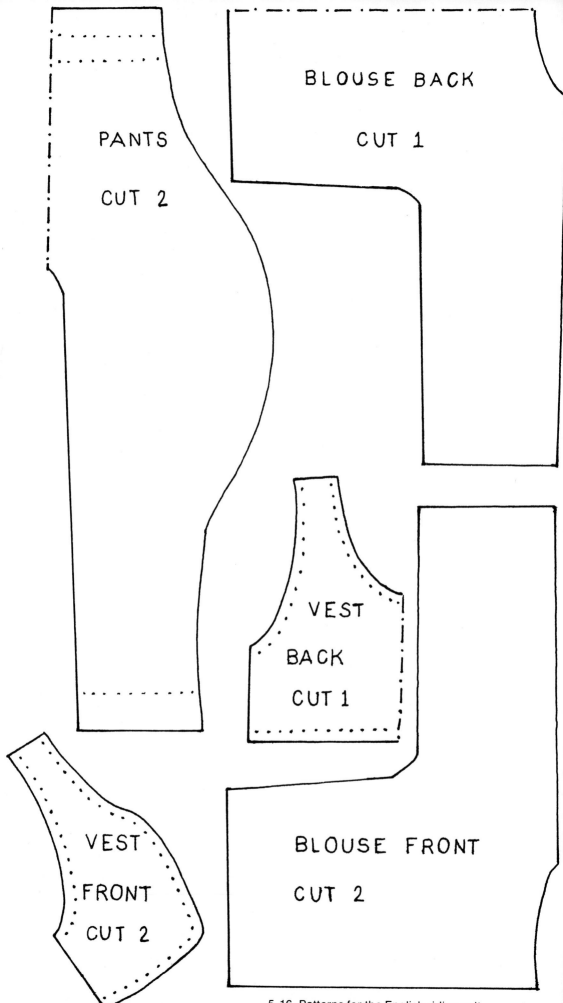

PANTS

CUT 2

BLOUSE BACK

CUT 1

VEST

BACK

CUT 1

VEST

FRONT

CUT 2

BLOUSE FRONT

CUT 2

5-16 Patterns for the English riding suit

EVENING GOWN, FUR COAT

The evening gown is cut from two solid colors, but you can use a print and a solid color. Brocade, velvet, or satin makes a nice choice of fabric. Decorate the gown with sequins, rhinestones, beads, or lace. The coat is made from imitation fur fabric.

MATERIALS

1/8 yard of imitation fur fabric for the coat.
A piece of fabric measuring 6 1/2 x 7 inches for the gown bodice.
A rectangle of fabric measuring 7 x 8 1/2 inches for the gown skirt.
A 27-inch length of 1/4-inch-wide ribbon for the waistband and ties.
Several sequins, rhinestones, or beads to decorate the bodice.
Two small snap closures.
Thread to match the fabrics.

5-17 Evening Gown and Fur Coat

The patterns are shown in Figure 5-18. Cut two bodice pieces, and a rectangle of fabric measuring 7 x 8 inches for the gown skirt. Cut two front coat pieces and one coat back piece. Transfer all markings to the wrong side of the fabrics.

Gown. Begin by stitching together the two bodice pieces (Figure 5-19). Align the bodice pieces, right sides together, and stitch together the upper curved edge and the two short ends of the piece. Turn right side out and press. Topstitch 1/8 inch within the upper curved edge and the short ends of the bodice.

To attach the skirt to the bodice, run a basting stitch 1/8 inch within and the length of one long edge of the skirt fabric. Draw up the stitching to match the length of the bodice waist, plus 1/2 inch (approximately 5 1/2 inches). Align the gathered edge of the skirt with the bodice waist edge: the skirt should overlap the back edges of the bodice 1/4 inch (Figure 3-25). Baste and then stitch the bodice skirt.

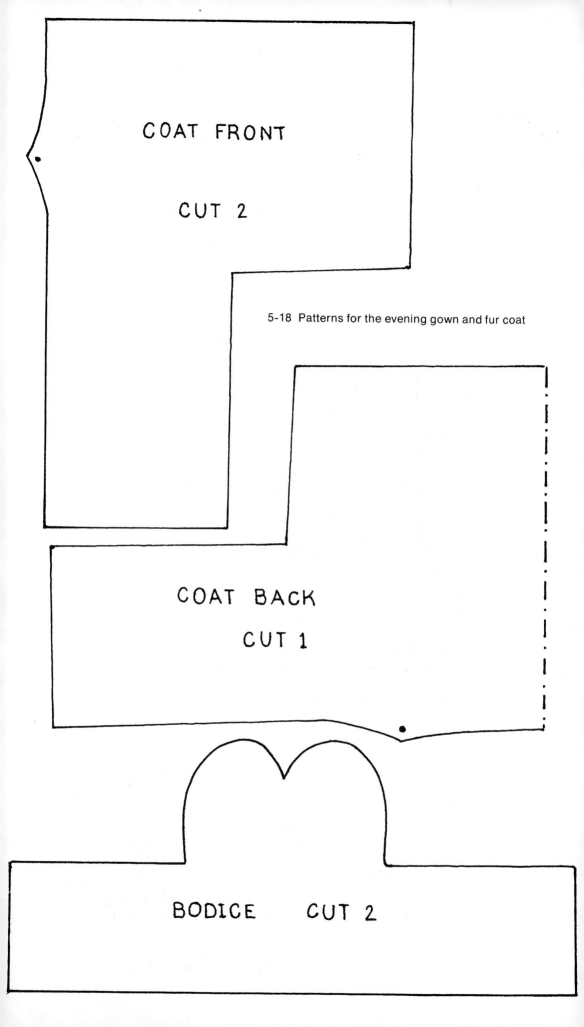

COAT FRONT

CUT 2

5-18 Patterns for the evening gown and fur coat

COAT BACK

CUT 1

BODICE   CUT 2

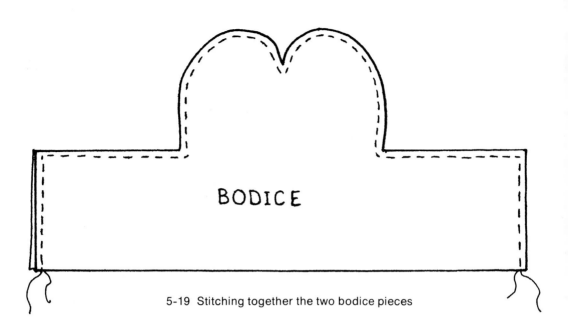

BODICE

5-19 Stitching together the two bodice pieces

To continue, stitch the back edge of the skirt together, from the base to within 1 inch of the bodice waist (Figure 5-7). Hem the raw edges of the opening below the waist. Hem the base of the skirt. Stitch two snap closures to the back of the bodice. Stitch a strap of satin ribbon 6 1/2 inches in length to each curve on the inside front of the bodice. These straps are tied around the neck of the doll to hold the bodice in place. Decorate the bodice of the gown with sequins, rhinestones, or beads. Tack a 14-inch length of satin ribbon to the underarm seams of the gown waist for a sash. Press.

Fur Coat. First align the two front coat pieces with the back piece, and stitch the shoulder seams from the dots at the neck edge of the coat to the ends of the sleeves. Stitch the underarm seams from the underside of the sleeves to the base of the coat. Hem the neck edge, the front opening edges, and the base of the coat. Carefully comb out any fur trapped in the seams. Placing a damp cloth between the fur fabric and the iron, press the coat.

The rest of the clothing in this chapter is designed for Mattel's action doll Big Jim. His measurements are: height, 9 1/2 inches; chest, 6 inches; waist, 4 1/2 inches; hips, 5 1/2 inches; length of arm, 3 inches; length of inner leg, 4 1/2 inches. Compare the measurements of your doll with these and alter the patterns if necessary.

SWIMSUIT

The swimsuit pattern can also be used for undershorts or tennis shorts.

MATERIALS

A piece of fabric 4 x 6 inches for the swimsuit.
A piece of 1/2-inch-wide by 5-inches-long bias
  tape.
One small snap closure.
Thread to match the fabric.

5-20 Men's Swimsuit

Using the pattern in Figure 5-21 as a guide, cut two swimsuit pieces.

To assemble this very simple garment, align the two pieces and stitch *one* side seam from the base of the leg to the waist. Stitch the second side seam from the base of the leg to within 1 inch of the waist. Hem the remaining edges of the opening in the side. Stitch the crotch seam. Hem the base of the legs. To create a waistband, bind the waist edge with bias tape. This procedure is illustrated in Figure 4-7. For more detailed information, turn to the section of chapter 6 that explains binding the neck edge of the princess gown. Stitch a snap closure to hold the waist edge of the slit closed. Press.

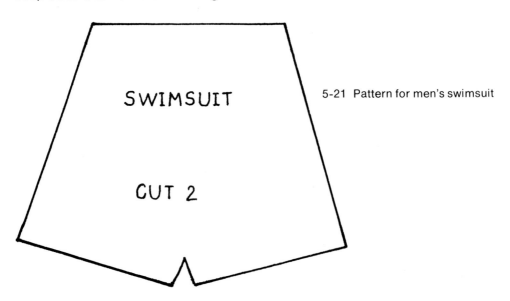

SWIMSUIT

CUT 2

5-21 Pattern for men's swimsuit

PAJAMAS

The pajamas pictured here are cut from plaid flannel. The edges are bound with bias tape in bright contrasting color. Other fabrics such as terry cloth, cotton, or satin would be equally attractive.

MATERIALS

1/8 yard of fabric for the pajama top and bottom.
1 yard of 1/2-inch-wide bias tape.
One snap closure.
Thread to match the fabric.

5-22 Men's Pajamas

Cut the appropriate number of pieces marked on the patterns in Figure 5-23. Transfer all markings to the wrong side of the fabrics.

Pajamas. Stitch together the top of the pajamas, stitching the back piece to the front pieces along the shoulder and the underarm seams (Figure 3-3). Hem the ends of the sleeves and the base of the garment. Finish the front opening edges and the neck edge by binding them with bias tape (Figure 4-7). This procedure is explained in chapter 6, binding the neck of the princess gown.

To make a tie, cut a strip of 1/2-inch-wide bias tape 12 inches long. Press the piece in half so it is 1/4 inch wide and the edges are tucked inside. Edgestitch together the edges opposite the fold. Hem the ends of the strip. Press. This tie will hold the top of the pajama top closed.

Pants. Align the two pants pieces, right sides together. Stitch *one* side seam from the base of the leg to the waist. Stitch the second side seam from the base of the leg to within 1 inch of the waist. Hem the raw edges of the opening in the side. Stitch the crotch seam. Hem the base of the legs. Bind off the waist edge with bias tape (Figure 4-7). Stitch a snap closure to the waist of the pajama bottoms so it will hold together the opening in the side. Press.

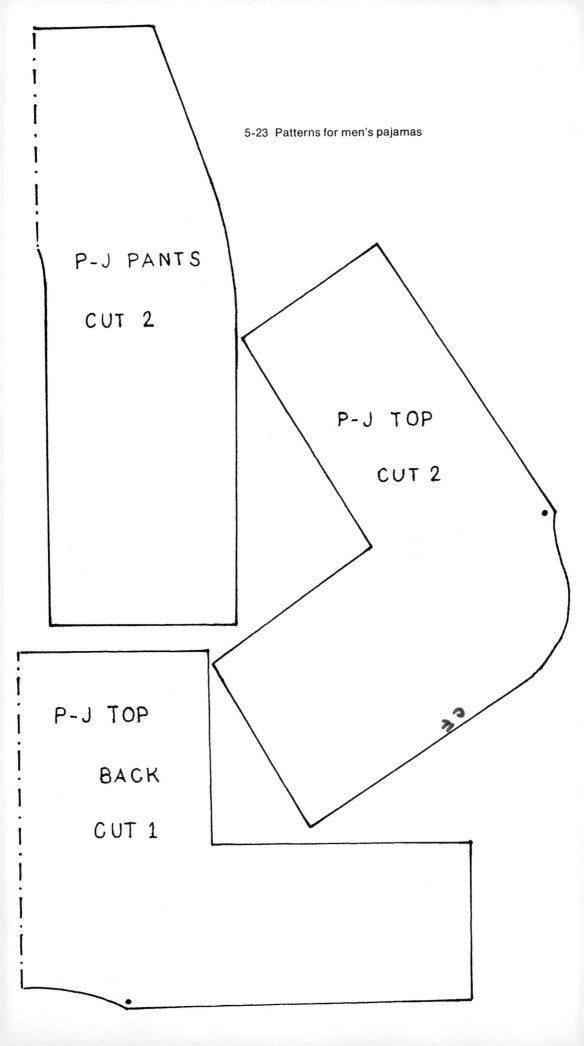

5-23 Patterns for men's pajamas

SPORTY OUTFIT

Jeans, a knit shirt, and loafers make up this traditional casual out-fit. Cut the jeans from blue or faded denim (a worn pair of discarded jeans is ideal). The shirt is cut from a cotton knit fabric, and the shoes are felt.

MATERIALS

1/8 yard of denim for the jeans.
A piece of knit fabric 6 x 8 inches for the shirt.
A piece of felt 5 x 5 inches for the shoes.
A 5-inch length of 1/2-inch-wide bias tape.
Two small snap closures.
Thread to match the fabrics.

5-24 Sporty Outfit

Using the patterns in Figure 5-25 as guides, cut two pants pieces, two shirt pieces, two shoe sides, two shoe uppers, two felt soles, and two soles from lightweight cardboard. Transfer the dot marked on the pants to the *wrong* side of *one* pants piece only. Transfer all other markings to the wrong side of the fabric.

Jeans. Begin with the pants piece marked with a dot. Cut a slit from the waist edge to the dot. Narrowly hem (1/4 inch) the edges of this slit. This piece is the pants front. Align the two pants pieces and then stitch the side seams from the base of the legs to the waist. Stitch the crotch seam. Hem the base of the legs. Bind the waist edge of the jeans with a blue bias tape (Figure 4-7). This procedure is explained in detail in chapter 6, in the section on the princess gown. Stitch two snap closures to the edges of the slit in the front of the pants so they will hold this opening closed. Press.

Shirt. The shirt can be made quickly and easily, and you may want to make several in different colors. With right sides together, align the two pieces. Stitch the shoulder seams from the dots marked at the neck edge to the ends of the sleeves (Figure 3-3). Stitch the under-arm seams. Hem the neck edge, the ends of the sleeves, and the base of the shirt. Press.

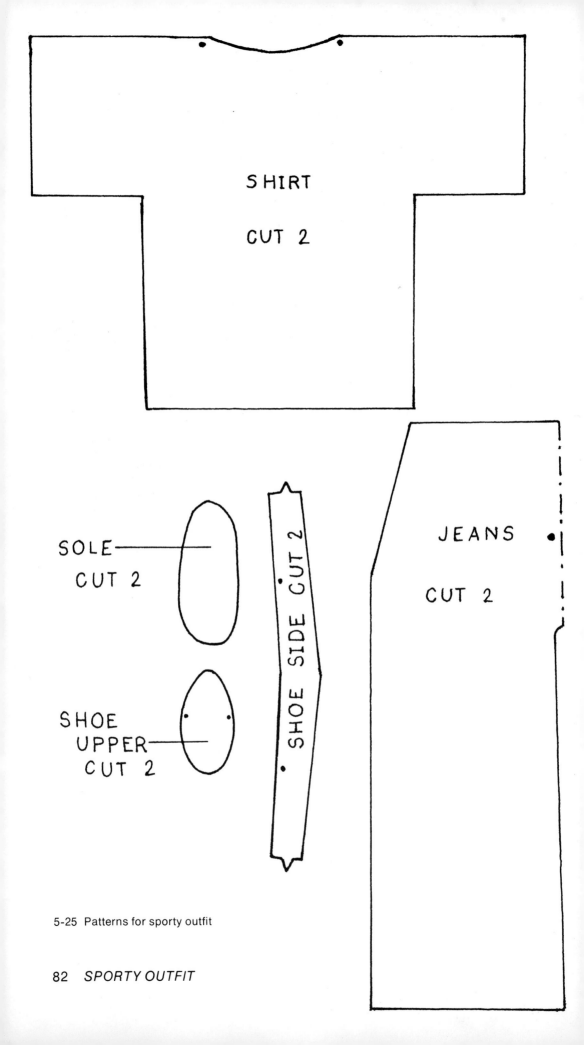

SHIRT

CUT 2

SOLE CUT 2

SHOE SIDE CUT 2

JEANS

CUT 2

SHOE UPPER CUT 2

5-25 Patterns for sporty outfit

Shoes. Before assembling the shoes refer to Figure 5-26. First, cut 1/8 inch from the perimeter of each cardboard sole. Glue a cardboard sole to each felt sole. Be sure you have a right sole and a left sole. Next take the strip of felt cut for the side of the shoe and stitch together the back notched edges so you have a hoop of fabric. Trim off the notch. Repeat for the second piece. Open out a hoop and insert a felt sole into the opening (the cardboard should be inside). By hand, stitch the sole to the lower edges of the side. Now fit the shoe upper over the toe of the shoe. Stitch the edges of the upper, between the dots, to the toe of the side (Figure 5-26d). Repeat and assemble the second shoe.

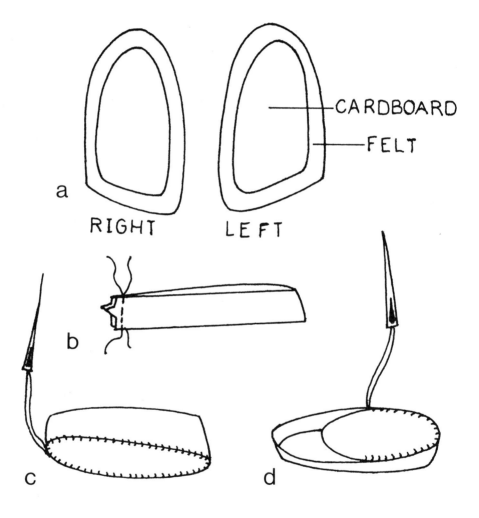

5-26 a. Gluing a cardboard sole to the felt sole
      b. Stitching together the notched back edge of
         the side of the shoe
      c. Stitching the sole to the side of the shoe
      d. Stitching the shoe upper over the toe of the shoe

DRESS SHIRT, TIE, PLAID SLACKS

The shirt is made from cotton, the tie from bias tape or grosgrain ribbon, and the slacks from wool plaid.

MATERIALS

1/8 yard of fabric for the slacks.
1/8 yard of fabric for the dress shirt.
A 14-inch length of 1/2-inch-wide bias tape for the tie and waistband.
Four small snap closures or two snaps and two buttons 1/8 inch in diameter.
Thread to match the fabrics.

5-27 Dress Shirt, Tie, and Plaid Slacks

Cut the appropriate number of pieces as indicated on the patterns in Figure 5-28. Using the pattern for the jeans (Figure 5-25), cut two pieces for the slacks. Transfer the dot marked on the jeans pattern to *one* slacks piece only. Transfer all other markings to the wrong side of the fabrics.

Slacks. To make the dress slacks, refer back to the previous section and follow the same procedure outlined for making the denim jeans.

Tie. Cut an 8-inch length of 1/2-inch bias tape or grosgrain ribbon. Fold the tape in half so it is 1/4 inch wide and the raw edges are tucked inside. Stitch the edges opposite the fold together. Hem the raw ends. Press.

Shirt. Begin by stitching the two front shirt pieces to the back piece along the shoulder seams, ending the stitching at the dots marked on the neck edge. Next, insert the sleeves (Figure 6-4b). Run a basting stitch 1/8 inch within the curved edge and between the dots marked on each sleeve. Align this edge with the edge of the armhole. Draw up the stitching, easing the sleeve to fit the armhole. Baste and then stitch the sleeve to the armhole. Stitch the underarm seams from the ends of the sleeves to the base of the shirt. Hem the front opening edges, the ends of the sleeves, and the base of the shirt.

To attach the collar, refer to Figure 3-16. Press 1/4 inch of the straight edge of one collar piece to the inside. Align the two collar pieces with one another and stitch the curved edge of the pair together. Turn the collar right side out and press. With right sides together, stitch the raw edge of the collar to the neck edge of the shirt. Press the seam toward the collar. Bring the folded edge of the collar to the inside, over the seam. Stitch the edge in place, by hand. Press the collar and topstitch it, close to the outer curved edge. To finish the shirt, stitch two snap closures evenly spaced to the front opening edges, or stitch two small buttons and make handworked buttonholes. Press the finished shirt.

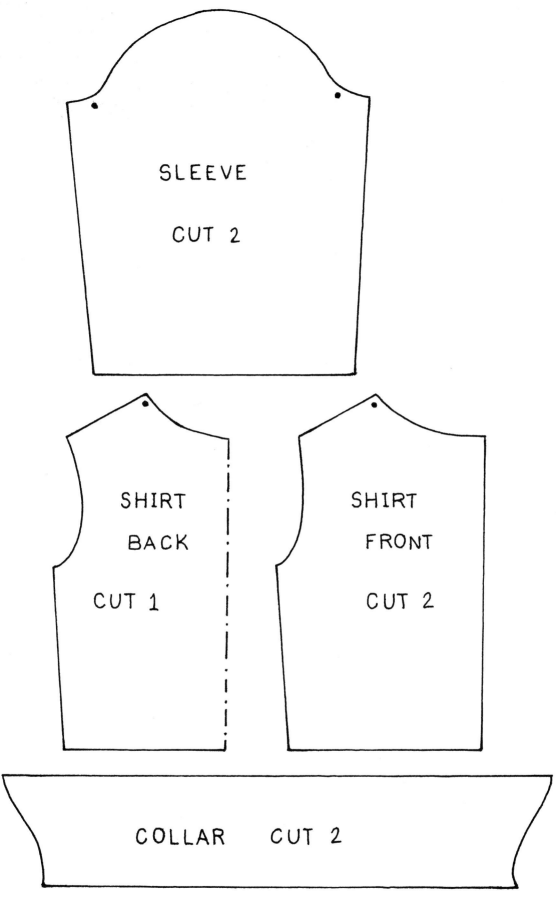

SLEEVE

CUT 2

SHIRT

BACK

CUT 1

SHIRT

FRONT

CUT 2

COLLAR   CUT 2

5-28 Patterns for the dress shirt

6 Costumes

The outfits in this chapter veer away from the more conventional clothing presented in the preceding chapters. The costumes can add variety to a doll's wardrobe, or they can be used to display a particular kind of doll. Included are outfits for a princess, cowgirl, ballerina, and Indian girl. The princess, cowgirl, and ballerina costumes were designed for an all-plastic doll distributed by Jolly Toys and made in Hong Kong. Her measurements are: height, 11 1/2 inches; chest, 6 1/2 inches; waist, 7 inches; hips, 7 inches; length of arm from shoulder to wrist, 3 1/4 inches; length of inner leg, 4 inches; length of foot, 1 1/2 inches; circumference of head, 10 inches. Before beginning the outfits, compare these measurements with your own doll and alter the patterns if necessary.

PRINCESS COSTUME

The outfit for the princess includes pantalets, slip, full-length dress, lacy pinafore, socks, and shoes.

6-1 Princess Costume

1/2 yard of soft pliable white fabric for the slip and
  pantalets.
1/2 yard of 44- or 45-inch-wide net fabric in a pastel color for stiffening the slip.
1/3 yard of delicate cotton print for the dress.
1/3 yard of lace fabric for the pinafore.
A 24-inch length of 1/2-inch-wide ribbon for the
  sash.
A scrap of white stretch fabric measuring 8 x 8
  inches, or a pair of white leotards you can cut up,
  to make socks.
A 9 x 9-inch square of black felt, for the shoes.
1 yard of 1-inch-wide gathered lace edging to trim
  the pinafore.
A 12-inch length of 3/4-inch-wide gathered lace
  edging to trim the pantalets.
A 27-inch length of 1/2-inch-wide lace edging to
  trim the slip.
A 17-inch length of 1/2-inch-wide single-fold bias
  tape, in a color compatible with the dress color.
A 12-inch length of 1/4-inch-wide elastic.
Five size 3/0 snaps.
Thread to match the fabrics.

Press all fabrics before cutting. The patterns for the Princess costume are shown in Figure 6-2a and b. Carefully note the cutting instructions marked on each pattern piece. Place edges on fold of fabric where indicated and cut the appropriate number of pieces
indicated. Cut one rectangle of slip fabric 6 x 25 inches and two
rectangles of net fabric each measuring 3 x 42 inches, for the slip.
Cut one rectangle of lace fabric measuring 6 x 22 inches for the
pinafore skirt. Cut one rectangle of dress fabric measuring 9 x 28
inches for the dress skirt. Transfer all markings from the patterns to
the *wrong* side of the fabric.

Pantalets. Select the two pantalet pieces, then refer to Figure 6-3
and align the two notched edges as illustrated. Stitch these edges
together from the waist to the crotch. Open out the piece and press
flat with the seam pressed open.
  Turn 1/4 inch of fabric along the waist edge to the inside. Press
and then stitch the edge in place. Turn 1/2 inch of fabric along this
same edge to the inside. Press and stitch very close to both edges of
the folded piece, forming a casing for elastic (Figure 3-7). Now cut a
6-inch length of 1/4-inch-wide elastic and thread the elastic through
the casing. Stitch the elastic securely to both ends of the casing.
Stitch together the remaining two notched edges for the pantalets,
from the waist edge to the crotch.
  Turn 1/4 inch of fabric along the base of each leg to the inside.
Press and then stitch the edges in place. Cut two pieces of 3/4-inch-
wide lace edging, each piece measuring the width of the base of the
leg (approximately 6 inches). Stitch a piece of lace to the right side of
the base of each leg.
  With the right sides of the fabric together, fold the legs, then stitch
the entire crotch seam, stitching the ends of the lace together as you
proceed (Figure 6-3b). Turn the finished pantalets right side out and
press.

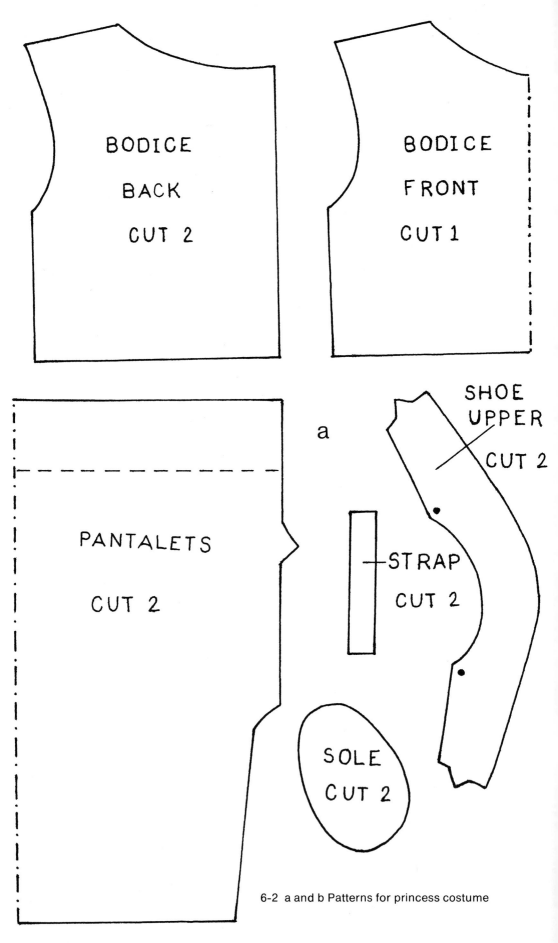

BODICE
BACK
CUT 2

BODICE
FRONT
CUT 1

a

SHOE
UPPER
CUT 2

PANTALETS

CUT 2

STRAP
CUT 2

SOLE
CUT 2

6-2 a and b Patterns for princess costume

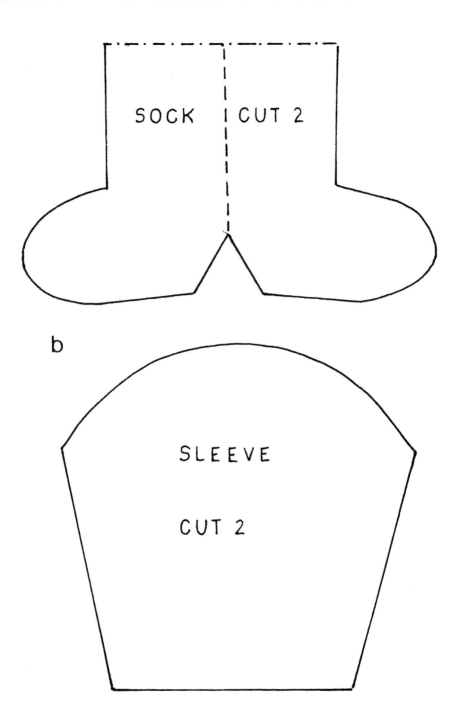

SOCK CUT 2

b

SLEEVE

CUT 2

Slip. To begin the slip, turn 1/4 inch of fabric along one long edge to the inside. Press and stitch this edge in place. Stitch a 27-inch length of 1/2-inch-wide lace edging to the right side of this edge. This will be the base of the slip.

Next make a casing for the elastic by turning to the inside 1/4 inch of fabric along the opposite long edge. Press then stitch the fabric edge in place. Turn 1/2 inch of fabric along the same edge to the inside and press. Stitch this edge in place, stitching very close to both edges of the pressed piece (Figure 3-7).

Baste together the long edge of the two pieces of net fabric, plac-

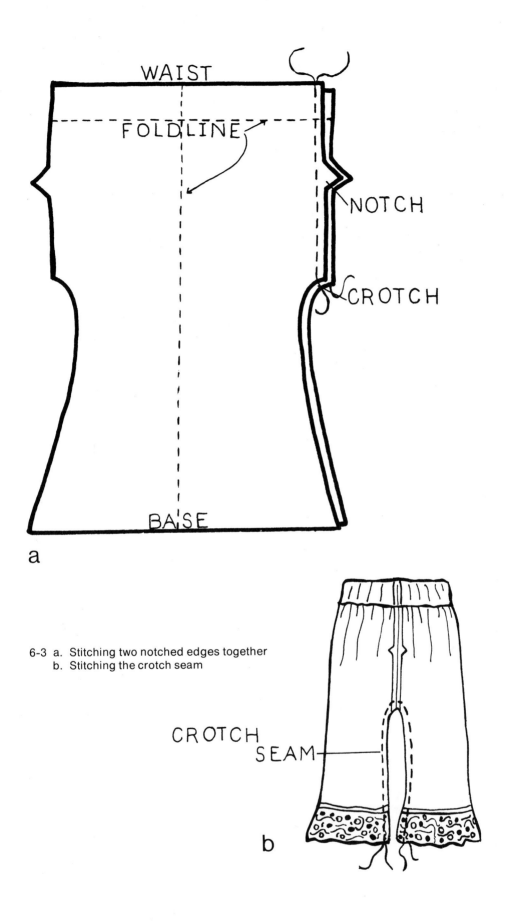

WAIST

FOLDLINE

NOTCH

CROTCH

BASE

a

6-3 a. Stitching two notched edges together
b. Stitching the crotch seam

CROTCH SEAM

b

ing the stitching 1/4 inch from the edge of the fabric. Draw up the stitching, gathering the net as you do so. Pin the gathered edge of the net to the wrong side of the slip 2 inches below the casing at the waist. Adjust the gathers so the net extends the full width of the slip and the gathers are uniform. Stitch the net to the slip, placing the line of stitching 1/4 inch within the basted edge of the net.

Thread the remaining 6-inch-long piece of elastic through the slip casing. Stitch the elastic to both ends of the casing. To finish, stitch the two short ends of the slip together, from the waist to the base of the lace, catching in the net. Turn the slip right side out and press carefully so as not to scorch the net.

Dress. Choose the piece cut for the bodice front and two pieces for the bodice back, then stitch the bodice front to the two back pieces at the shoulder seams (Figure 6-4a).

To make a neat attractive finish, the collar, the open edges at the back of the dress, and the wrist edges of the sleeves are bound with bias tape. The steps for this procedure are illustrated in Figure 4-7. Study the illustration before proceeding.

Cut a piece of bias tape measuring the length of the bodice neck edge, plus 1/2 inch. Unfold one edge of the tape. Align the edge of the right side of the unfolded raw edge of the tape with the edge of the wrong side of the dress neck. One quarter inch of tape should extend beyond each end of the neck edge. Baste and then stitch the tape to the bodice, keeping the stitching close to the edge of the fabric and within the foldline of the tape. Do *not* unfold the remaining tape. Bend the bias tape over the neck edge to the right side of the dress. The wrong side of the tape and right side of the dress should now be flush with one another. Stitch the tape to the dress, placing the line of stitching very close to the lower edge of the tape. Turn the ends of the tape, which extend beyond the neck, under and to the inside. Stitch them in place.

Sleeves are next. Following the above procedure, bind the wrist edge of each sleeve with bias tape. Then run a basting stitch the length of and 1/8 inch within the shoulder edge of each sleeve. Draw up this stitching so the sleeve is slightly gathered. Pin and then baste a sleeve to each armhole opening. Adjust the gathers so they are distributed evenly. Stitch the sleeves to the bodice (Figure 6-4b).

Stitch the two underarm seams from the base of the bodice to the wrist edges of the sleeves.

To attach the skirt to the bodice, begin by stitching a line of basting 1/4 inch within one long edge of the rectangular piece of skirt fabric. Turn 1/4 inch of fabric along the opposite long edge to the inside. Press and stitch this edge in place. Now draw up the basting thread so that the skirt is tightly gathered. With right sides together, pin the gathered edge of the skirt to the lower edge of the bodice. Adjust the gathers so that they are uniform. Baste and then stitch the skirt to the bodice (Figure 3-25). Stitch the back of the skirt together from the lower edge to 2 inches from the point where the skirt is attached to the bodice (Figure 5-7).

Now, following the same procedure used for the neck edge and wrists, bind the open edges of the back of the dress with bias tape. Cut a piece of bias tape measuring the length of the back open edge plus 1/2 inch to overlap at the neck edge. Stitch the tape in place and stitch the overlapping edges to the inside. Stitch three snaps to the bound edges of the back opening, spacing them an inch apart.

Try the dress on the doll. Turn up an appropriate hem and pin it in place. Using a hemming stitch, attach the hem in place. Press the dress.

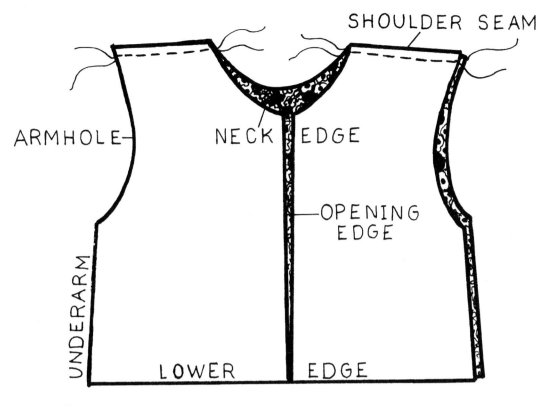

SHOULDER SEAM

ARMHOLE—

NECK EDGE

—OPENING
EDGE

UNDERARM

LOWER   EDGE

a

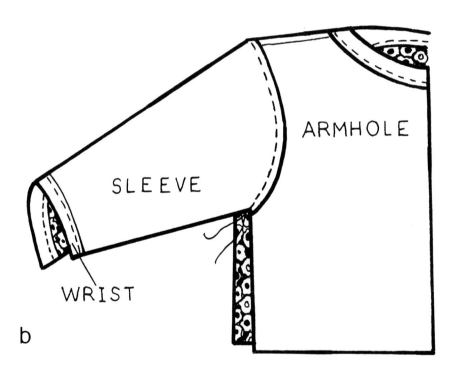

ARMHOLE

SLEEVE

WRIST

b

6-4 a. Stitching the front to the back at
          the shoulder seams
      b. Stitching the sleeve to the armhole

Pinafore. Stitch the front bodice piece to the two back bodice pieces at the shoulder seams as illustrated in Figure 6-4a. Stitch the underarm seams from the base of the bodice to the lower edge of the armholes.

By hand, using tiny stitches, hem the neck edge and the armhole edges, turning 3/8 inch of hem to the inside along each of the edges.

Cut two pieces of 1-inch-wide by 6-inch-long gathered lace edging. Narrowly hem the raw ends of these two pieces. Pin a piece of lace edging to the right side of each armhole edge, beginning and ending 1/4 inch from the underarm seam. Stitch the lace to the bodice.

Turn 1/4 inch of fabric to the inside along one long edge of the rectangular piece of lace fabric you are using for the pinafore skirt. Press and stitch this edge in place. Cut a piece of 1-inch-wide lace edging the length of this edge (approximately 22 inches). Stitch the lace to the right side of the turned edge. Stitch a line of basting 1/4 inch from the opposite long edge of the pinafore skirt. Draw up the stitching so the edge is gathered. Pin the right side of the gathered edge to the right side of the bodice. Adjust the gathers. Baste and then stitch the skirt to the bodice (Figure 3-25). Carefully hem the open back edges of the pinafore from the neck to the lower edge of the skirt.

Stitch two size 3/0 snaps to the pinafore bodice, placing one at the neck and the other an inch below the first.

Now the two loops which hold the sash in place are added. Begin by stitching a loop of doubled sewing thread, from the inside, through the pinafore waist at one underarm seam, and back through the fabric 5/8 inch above the waist. Knot the thread on the inside, making sure it is loose enough for the sash to pass through the loop. Stitch a second loop to the remaining underarm seam.

Fold the ribbon for the sash in half to find the center, then place the center point at the center front of the bodice, with the lower edge of the sash flush with the waist edge. Stitch the sash to the bodice front at the point with a couple of concealed stitches. Thread the ends of the ribbon through the loops at the underarm seams. When the pinafore is on the doll, tie the sash in a large bow at the back.

Socks. Fold one sock piece along the fold line marked on the fabric. You now have a double layer of fabric (Figure 6-5). Now fold the piece again so that the toes are together, and you have four layers of fabric. Stitch from the top of the sock, down the front, around the toe, along the base of the foot, ending at the point where the fold begins. Turn the sock right side out. Turn 1/2 inch of fabric around the upper edge to the inside. Tack this edge to the seam with one or two stitches to hold it in place. Repeat and make the second sock.

Shoes. To begin the shoes, use the sole pattern for a guide, and cut two soles from cardboard. Trim 1/8 inch from the perimeter of each of the cardboard pieces. With white glue, cloth glue, or liquid rubber, glue a cardboard sole to the center of each black felt sole, making sure you have a right and a left sole (Figure 6-6 illustrates the steps in shoe construction).

Next, stitch close to the upper edge of each shoe piece, as indicated by the dots marked on the pieces. Fold one upper shoe piece so that the notched ends of the piece are aligned. Stitch these ends together by hand with an overcast stitch. Trim the notch off, so that the seam is even. Repeat with the second shoe. Overcast stitch a sole to the lower edge of each shoe piece. The cardboard insert should be on the inside of the shoe. To finish, stitch the strap to the upper edge of the shoe, stitching an end to each dot marked on the inside edge.

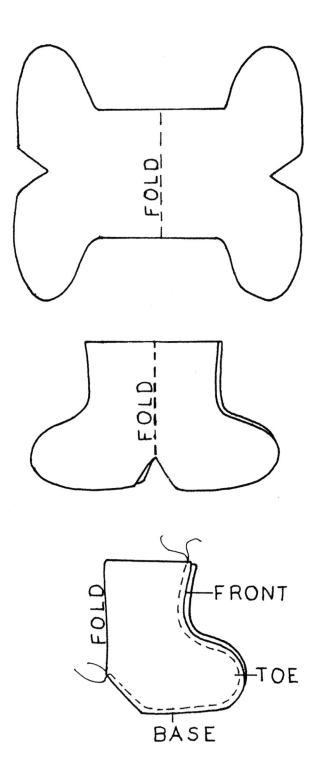

6-5 Folding and stitching one sock

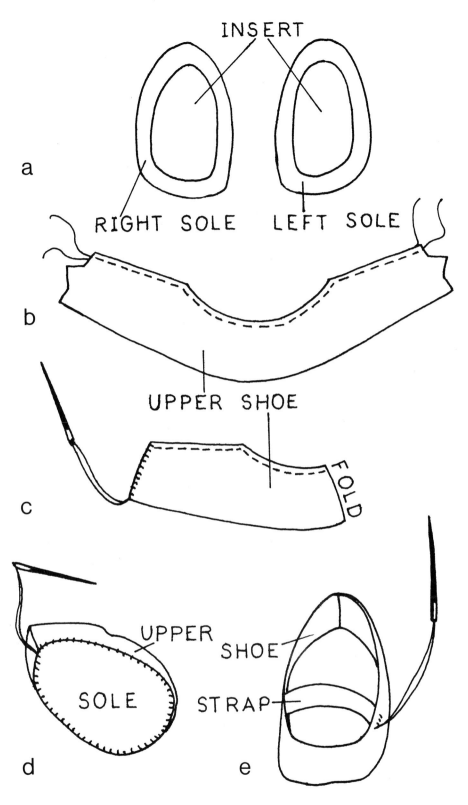

6-6 a. Gluing a cardboard insert to the right and
        left sole
     b. Stitching close to the upper edge of each shoe

     c. Stitching notched ends together. (Notches
        are to be trimmed off)
     d. Overcast stitching upper shoe to sole
     e. Stitching the strap to the upper shoe

COWGIRL COSTUME

The cowgirl outfit includes underpants, slacks, blouse, vest, hat, socks, and boots.

6-7 Cowgirl Costume

MATERIALS

1/3 yard of cotton fabric, such as kettle cloth, for the vest and slacks.

1/3 yard of plaid cotton flannel for the blouse.

A 7 x 9-inch rectangle of russet-colored felt for the hat and boots.

An 8 x 10-inch scrap of lightweight white cotton fabric for the underpants.

A scrap of white stretch fabric measuring at least 8 x 8 inches, or a pair of discarded leotards, for the socks.

An 18-inch length of 1/2-inch-wide single fold bias tape to trim the blouse.

A 12-inch length of 1/4-inch-wide elastic.

Two size 3/0 snaps.

Scraps of yellow felt to decorate the vest.

A 14-inch length of rawhide, or similar material, for a hatband.

Thread to match the fabrics.

Press fabrics before cutting. The patterns for the cowgirl outfit are shown in Figure 6-8a, b, and c. Cut the appropriate number of pieces marked on the pattern from the fabrics you have chosen. For socks, use the pattern in Figure 6-2b. Cut a rectangle of felt 1 1/4 x 11 inches for the crown of the hat. Transfer all markings to the wrong side of the fabric.

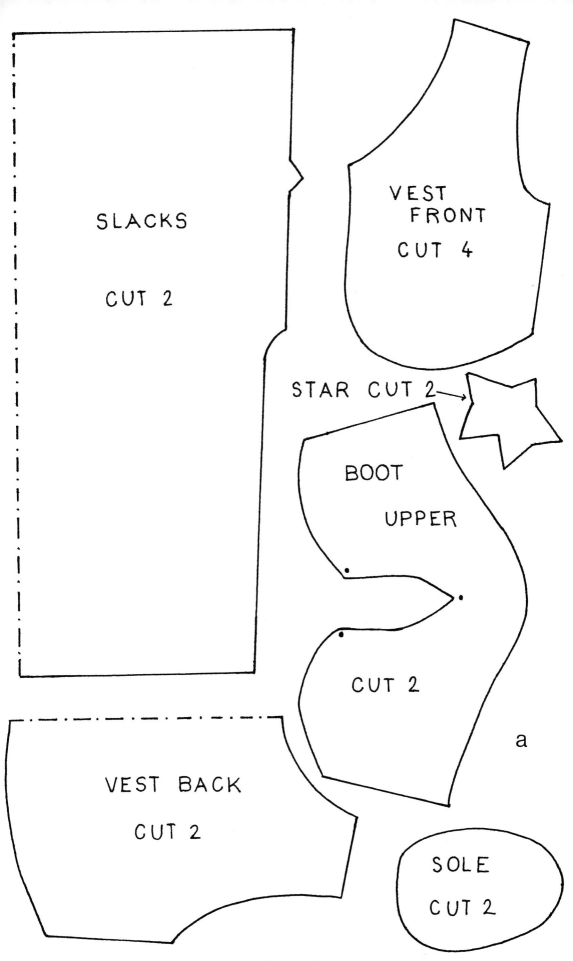

SLACKS

CUT 2

VEST
FRONT
CUT 4

STAR CUT 2 →

BOOT

UPPER

CUT 2

a

VEST BACK

CUT 2

SOLE

CUT 2

6-8 a, b, and c Patterns for cowgirl costume

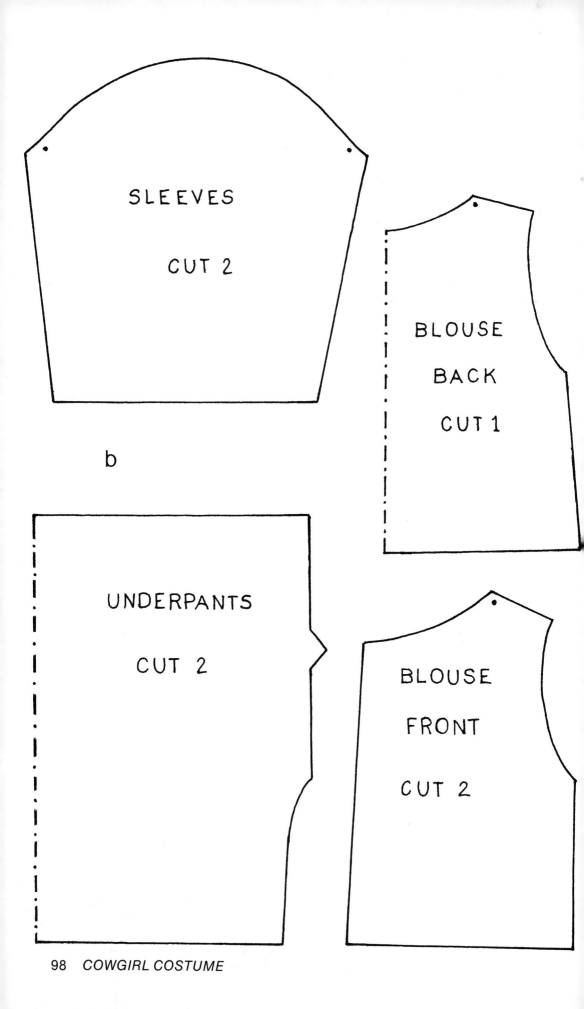

SLEEVES

CUT 2

b

BLOUSE

BACK

CUT 1

UNDERPANTS

CUT 2

BLOUSE

FRONT

CUT 2

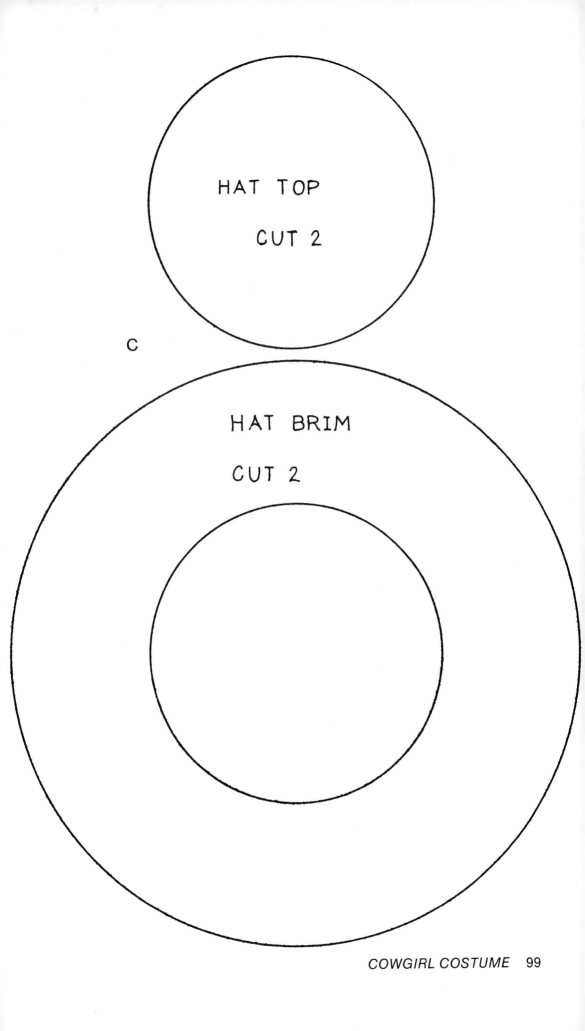

HAT TOP

CUT 2

C

HAT BRIM

CUT 2

Underpants. Align the two pieces of underpants fabric with the notched edges together (Figure 6-3a). Stitch. Open out the piece and press flat with the seam pressed open. Turn 1/4 inch of fabric along the waist edge to the inside. Press and stitch this edge in place. Turn 1/2 inch of fabric along the same edge to the inside, press, and then stitch very close to both edges of this folded piece (Figure 3-7), forming a casing for the elastic. Cut a 6-inch length of 1/4-inch-wide elastic. Thread the elastic through the casing, stitching it securely to both ends of the casing. Stitch the remaining two notched edges together from the waist to the crotch.

Turn 1/4 inch of fabric to the inside along the base of each leg. Press and stitch these edges in place. Stitch the entire crotch seam (Figure 6-3b). Turn the underpants right side out and try them on the doll. Pin up a suitable hem. Remove the pants and stitch the hem in place. Press the garment.

Slacks. The slacks are made by following the same procedure outlined for the underpants, except, of course, you use fabric you cut for the slacks. When you have finished, topstitch the base of the slacks legs 1/8 inch from the edge to give a decorative western look.

Blouse. The blouse is assembled from five pieces. Stitch the two blouse front pieces to the back piece at the shoulder seam (Figure 6-4a shows the procedure, stitching one front piece to two back pieces, but the principle is the same). Now turn and then press 1/4-inch of fabric along the blouse front open edges to the inside. Stitch them in place and turn another 1/4 inch of fabric along the same edges to the inside. Press and stitch these edges in place.

The neck edge of the blouse is bound with bias tape to create a mock turtleneck. Cut a piece of bias tape measuring the length of the neck edge plus 1/2 inch. Open out one folded edge of the tape and pin the right side of the unfolded raw edge of the tape to the wrong side of the neck edge (Figure 4-7).

One quarter inch of tape should extend beyond the neck edge at the front of the blouse. Stitch the tape to the blouse. Fold the tape over the neck edge so that the wrong side of the tape and the right side of the blouse are together. Do not unfold the second edge of the tape. Stitch the tape to the blouse, placing a line of stitching close to both edges of the tape. Turn the overlap of tape to the inside of the blouse and stitch it in place.

Bind the wrist edge of each sleeve, following the same procedure explained above.

Now stitch a line of basting within 1/4 inch of the shoulder edge of each sleeve. Draw up this stitching so that the sleeves are slightly gathered. Baste the gathered edge of the sleeves to the armhole openings of the shirt, adjusting the gathers so they are uniform and keep the right sides of the fabric together. Stitch the sleeves to the blouse (Figure 6-4b).

Next stitch the underarm seams of the blouse from the lower edge of the blouse to the sleeve wrists. Turn 1/4-inch of fabric around the lower edge of the blouse to the inside. Press and stitch this edge in place. Hem the blouse by turning an additional 1/4 inch of fabric to the inside and stitch it in place with a hemming stitch. Stitch two size 3/0 snaps to the blouse front, placing one at the neck edge and another an inch below the first.

Vest. The vest has duplicate lining pieces front and back, which allows for a neat finish for the neck and armhole edges. With right sides together, stitch the two back pieces to one another along the neck, the armhole, and the lower edges of the pieces (Figure 6-9a).

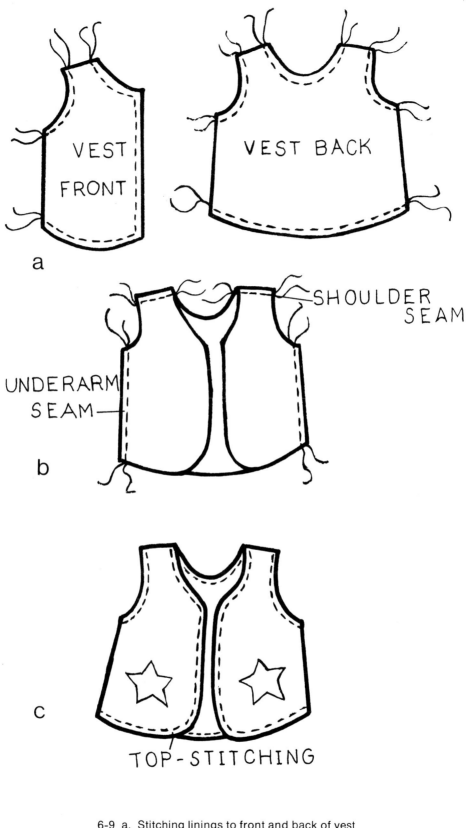

VEST FRONT

VEST BACK

a

SHOULDER SEAM

UNDERARM SEAM

b

c

TOP-STITCHING

6-9 a. Stitching linings to front and back of vest
     b. Stitching vest front to back at shoulder and
        underarm seams
     c. Topstitching the vest

The sides and shoulders are left unstitched. In the same manner, stitch each of the two front pieces to a lining piece. In this case, stitch the front as well as the neck, the armhole, and lower edge together.

Turn the three pieces right side out. Stitch the fronts of the vest to the back at the shoulder seams. Stitch the side seams of the vest to the back at the underarm seams. Stitch the side seams of the vest from the armhole to the lower edge. Topstitch around the entire perimeter of the garment, including the armhole openings, for a decorative finish. Using a cloth glue, glue a felt star to each front side of the vest as indicated. Press.

Socks. Directions for the socks are exactly the same as for the princess' socks. Follow the instructions step by step.

Boots. To begin the boots, use the sole pattern as a guide and cut two cardboard soles. Use cardboard the thickness of a cereal box. Trim 1/8 inch from the perimeter of the cardboard soles. Glue a sole to the center of each felt sole, making sure you have a right and a left sole (Figure 6-6a).

Next take one of the felt boot uppers, and fold it so that the two notched back edges of the piece are evenly aligned. Stitch this edge securely together, using an overcast stitch. Trim off the notches so that the seam is even. Next align the front edges of the boot, and overcast stitch them together from the dot to the point where they join one another. Overcast stitch the sole to the lower edge of the boot. To finish, overcast stitch along the upper edges. Repeat and assemble the second boot.

Hat. If the felt you have chosen for the hat is thick and holds its shape, you don't have to double the pieces, but if the felt is of a limp quality, it will be necessary to double the pieces. To begin, glue each piece to its matching piece. When the glue is thoroughly dry, topstitch close to the edges (both inner and outer) placing the lines of stitching 1/4 inch within the edges. Overlap and glue the ends of the strip of fabric you are using for the crown 1 inch (Figure 6-10). Glue the top of the hat over one open end of the crown. Glue the brim to the lower edge of the other open end. When the hat is dry, tie the rawhide hatband around the crown. Roll up the brim, and with a few stitches, attach it to the crown.

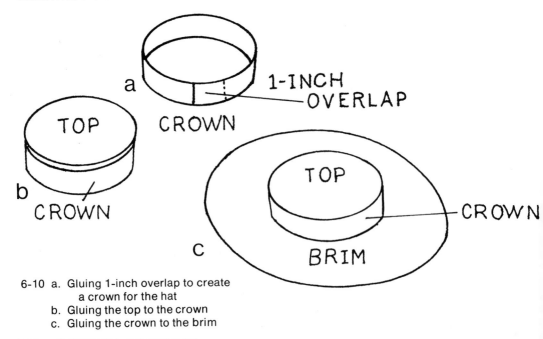

6-10 a. Gluing 1-inch overlap to create
      a crown for the hat
   b. Gluing the top to the crown
   c. Gluing the crown to the brim

BALLERINA COSTUME

This outfit is very popular with young girls who aspire to become ballerinas. The costume consists of a short dress with a lacy overskirt, leotards, and ballerina slippers. A stretchable knit fabric of the kind used for panty hose is necessary for the leotards. Use lace fabric for the overskirt. The shoes are cut from felt. The dress can be cut from cotton, silk, satin, or any number of fabrics.

6-11 Ballerina Costume

MATERIALS

1/8 yard of fabric for the dress.
A rectangle of lace fabric measuring 4 1/4 x 25
   inches for the overskirt.
1/8 yard of knit fabric for the leotards.
A piece of felt 4 x 6 inches for the shoes.
A 6-inch length of 1/2-inch-wide bias tape for
   dress straps.
Two small snap closures.
Two 7-inch lengths of 1/4-inch-wide elastic.
Thread to match the fabrics.

Refer to Figure 6-12 which shows the patterns for the ballerina costume. Cut the appropriate number of pieces as marked on the patterns. Cut a rectangle of dress fabric measuring 4 x 15 inches for the skirt. Cut a rectangle of lace fabric measuring 4 1/2 x 25 inches for the overskirt. Using the sole pattern as a guide, cut two additional soles from lightweight cardboard. Transfer the dots to the right side of the shoe uppers. Transfer all other markings to the wrong side of the fabric.

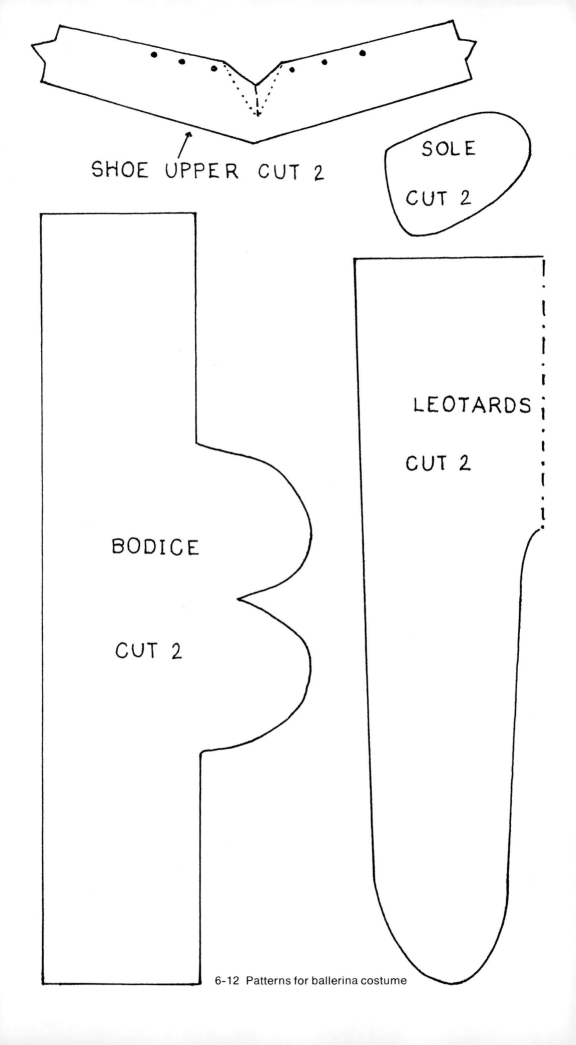

SHOE UPPER CUT 2

SOLE CUT 2

BODICE CUT 2

LEOTARDS CUT 2

6-12 Patterns for ballerina costume

Leotards. Align the two pieces of fabric for the leotards, right sides together, and stitch *one* side seam from the toe to the waist. Open out the leotard and press it open. Turn, press to the inside, and stitch 1/4 inch of fabric along the waist edge. Turn an additional 1/2 inch of fabric along this same edge to the inside. Press and stitch close to both edges of this folded piece (Figure 3-7). Thread a 7-inch length of elastic through the casing, then stitch the ends of the elastic to the ends of the casing. Fold the leotards closed and stitch the second side seam from the toe to the waist, stitching the ends of the casing together as you proceed. Stitch the crotch seam, stitching the inner toe and inner leg seams. Turn the leotard right side out. Place a damp cloth between the fabric and the iron and press.

Dress. Align the two bodice pieces then stitch them together along the curved edge and the short ends of the pieces (Figure 5-19). Turn the bodice right side out and topstitch along these same edges.

Now take the piece of fabric you cut for the skirt and run a line of basting stitches 1/8 inch within and the length of one long edge. Draw up this stitching, gathering the edge to match the bodice length of the waist (approximately 8 inches). Add 1/2 inch to this measurement to allow the skirt to overlap the edges of the bodice 1/4 inch (Figure 3-25). Baste and then stitch the gathered edge of the skirt to the waist edge of the bodice. Press the skirt down. Stitch the back seam of the skirt to within 1 inch of the bodice waist (Figure 5-7). Hem the raw edges of the opening in the seam below the waist. Hem the base of the skirt. Stitch snap closures to the upper edge and waist at the bodice back.

Straps for the ballerina dress can be made from 1/4-inch-wide satin ribbon, or 1/2-inch-wide single fold bias tape can be used if you don't have ribbon. Try the dress on the doll and measure over the shoulder, between the bodice front and back. Add 1 inch to this measurement to allow for a hem and stitching. Using this measurement, cut two lengths of bias tape. Fold the pieces in half, so they are 1/4 inch wide. Stitch the edges opposite the fold together. Hem the ends. Stitch one end of each strap on each side of the inside front of the bodice. Stitch the remaining ends to the back of the bodice, one on each side. Press.

Overskirt. The overskirt is a hoop of gathered lace fabric. To begin, turn, press, and stitch 1/4 inch of fabric along one long edge to the inside. Turn and press to the inside 1/2 inch of fabric along this same edge. To create a casing for elastic stitch close to both edges of this folded piece (Figure 3-7). Thread a 7-inch length of elastic through the casing and stitch the ends of the elastic to the ends of the casing. Stitch the narrow ends of the lace fabric together. Hem the base of the overskirt. Press. The lace overskirt fits over the dress.

Slippers. Begin the slippers by trimming 1/8 inch from the perimeters of the cardboard soles. Glue a cardboard sole to each felt sole. Be sure you have a right and a left sole (Figure 6-6). Next stitch the dart marked on the inside toe of each felt upper. Stitch together the notched back edges. Open out the base of an upper and slip a felt sole (cardboard on the inside) into the opening. Stitch the edge of the upper to the edge of the sole. Lastly, for laces, cut two 24-inch lengths of embroidery thread. Crisscross stitch these threads across the toe of each shoe, using the dots marked there for guides. When you put the shoes on the doll, continue to crisscross the thread around her ankle, finishing with a bow tied in front, just below the knee.

INDIAN GIRL COSTUME

This costume was designed for a dark-skinned, dark-eyed doll, made in Hong Kong, manufacturer unknown. Her measurements are: height, 9 inches; chest, 6 1/2 inches; waist, 6 1/2 inches; hips, 7 inches; length of arm to the wrist, 3 inches; circumference of head, 9 inches. If your doll's measurements vary from these, alter the patterns as explained in chapter 1.

Included in the Indian costume is a fringed beaded dress, a headband, and moccasins. To obtain the soft leathery look of doeskin, use suede cloth or a soft brown velour for the dress. The moccasins and headband must be cut from felt.

6-13 Indian Girl Costume

MATERIALS

1/4 yard of fabric for the dress.
A piece of felt 9 x 12 inches for the headband and
  moccasins.
A 14-inch length of 1/4-inch-wide rawhide for the
  tie at the waist.
Several beads with 1/8-inch diameters to decorate
  the dress and headband. And a feather approxi-
  mately 3 1/2 inches in length for the headband.
Two small snaps.
Thread to match the fabrics.

The patterns for the Indian costume are shown in Figure 6-14. Cut the appropriate number of pieces as marked on the patterns. Cut two strips of felt, each measuring 3/4 x 9 1/2 inches, for the headband. Cut two additional soles from lightweight cardboard. Transfer the dots for placement of the beads, and transfer the dashed lines for cutting the fringe to the right side of the dress and to the shoe uppers. Transfer the X to the wrong side of *one* dress piece only. Transfer all other markings to the wrong side of the fabrics.

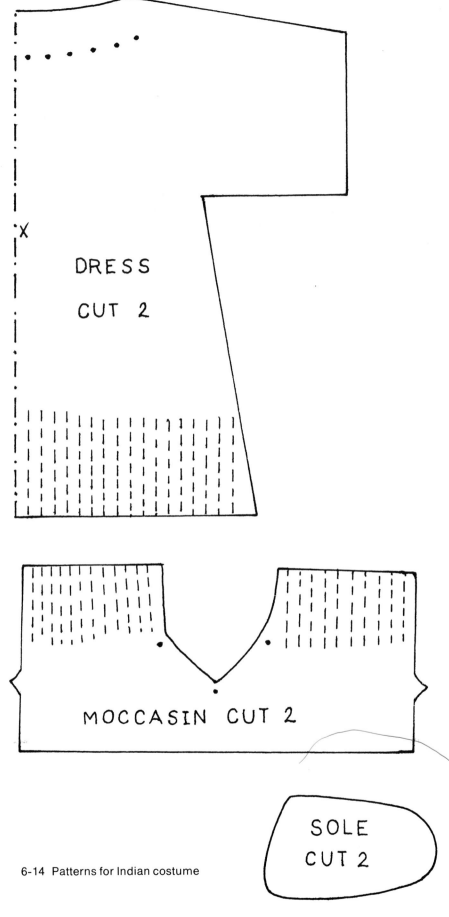

X

DRESS

CUT 2

MOCCASIN CUT 2

SOLE

CUT 2

6-14 Patterns for Indian costume

Dress. The dress is simply constructed; its charm is in the surface decoration. Take the back dress piece marked with an X and cut a slit from the neck edge to the X. Now align the two dress pieces and stitch the shoulder seams from the dots marked at the neck edge to the ends of the sleeves. Stitch the underarm seams to the base of the dress. Hem the neck edge, the edges of the slit, and the ends of the sleeves.

Before cutting the fringe, encircle the base of the dress with topstitching 1/8 inch above the slashed lines. Cut the fringe along the dashed lines, but take care not to cut across the line of topstitching.

Next stitch a snap closure to the neck edge of the slit, and stitch a second snap 3/4 inch below the first. Press the dress. Stitch colored beads to the points on the front of the dress marked with dots (if you prefer, stitch a more intricate beaded design of your own). Use clear nylon thread to conceal the stitching. When the dress is on the doll, tie the length of rawhide around her waist.

Moccasins. The moccasins are made much the same way as the other shoes in this chapter. First trim 1/8 inch from the perimeter of each cardboard sole. Glue a cardboard sole to each felt sole, taking care to have a right and left sole (Figure 6-6). Next, overcast stitch together the notched back edges of each upper. Trim off the notches. The shoes will turn out better if the stitching is done by hand. Stitch together the toe seam of each upper, between the dots. Then, open out the base of the upper and insert the felt sole (cardboard on the inside) into the opening. Stitch the edge of the base of the upper to the edge of the sole. Lastly, carefully cut along the dashed lines marked for cutting the fringe. Fold the fringe down over the sides of the moccasins.

Headband. The headband is made from two strips of felt topstitched together. A contrasting color of thread and a zigzag stitch create an interesting decorative effect. Align the two strips with one another and topstitch the long edges of the pair together. Try the band on the doll. Overlap the back edges for an accurate fit. Remove the band and stitch the overlapped ends together. Decorate the headband with a row of beads stitched to the fabric. As a finishing touch, stitch a feather to the headband.

There are an infinite number of costumes, ancient and traditional, from Japan, Switzerland, India—using the information offered here, you could design hundreds of patterns for your dolls.

Glossary

Armhole: An opening in an unfinished garment into which the sleeve fits.

Baste: To use a long, loose stitch (hand or machine) to hold two edges together temporarily or to gather an edge. The bastings are removed when the edge is permanently stitched.

Bias Tape: Precut and prefolded fabric strip used for finishing raw edges and making straps or casings.

Binding: A method of finishing an edge by wrapping it with a strip of fabric.

Bodice: That part of a gown, dress, etc., which is above the waist.

Casing: A tunnel of fabric through which elastic, ribbon, or string is threaded.

Circumference: The outer edge of a circle.

Closure: A button, snap, zipper, or tie which fastens or holds a garment in place.

Easing: Drawing up or stretching a fabric edge to fit another edge of a different length.

Facing: A piece of fabric that fits on the inside of a garment and finishes the edge to which it is attached.

Finish: To hem, bind, or in some way prepare a raw edge so it will not fray.

Edge: The boundary of a piece of fabric.

Gathering: Drawing up a piece of fabric along a line of basting so it is softly ruffled.

Hem: An edge of fabric (usually the base of a skirt, sleeve, etc.) that is folded and stitched to the inside to finish the edge. Half an inch of fabric is allowed for hems in this book.

Inside: The side of the fabric which will not be visible when the garment is finished.

Nap: A plushy, soft, or fuzzy surface texture characteristic of some fabrics such as velvet or fake fur.

Needles: Needles are necessary for hand or machine stitching. I recommend ball-point needles for machine sewing, small slender needles for hand sewing, and large needles for embroidery.

Perimeter: The outer edge.

Pins and Cushion: Straight pins are necessary to hold patterns and fabrics in place. Colorful beaded heads on pins make them easy to spot and less likely to be left in the fabrics. Any stuffed cushion is helpful to keep pins in one place and accessible.

Raw Edge: The perimeter of a piece of fabric before it has been finished.

Remnant: Small piece of fabric usually left over from a bolt and sold at a reduced price.

Right Side: The side of fabric that is visible when a garment is finished.

Seam: A seam is a line of stitching that holds two or more edges of fabric together. One quarter inch of fabric is suggested for seams in this book.

Stitch: To bind together two pieces of fabric with thread.

Topstitch: To stitch on the right side of the fabric, usually close to a seam or edge.

Waistband: A strip of fabric stitched to the upper edge of a skirt or trousers, fitting snugly around a doll's waist.

Wrong Side: The side of the fabric that is not visible when the garment is finished.

Yard: A yard is a length of material 36 inches long. (It should be *at least* 36 inches wide as well.)

Zigzag: A machine stitch useful for finishing a seam, binding a raw edge, or for decorative purposes.

Index